"I walked outside one day and saw his bong sitting on top of the bird book. That's when I knew something was up."

- Owen Reiser

Introduction

If you really want help identifying birds, this is not a good tool. This guidebook is just a recollection of all the birds my brother, **Owen**, and I were able to find in one year with little to no knowledge about birds or birding. If you're looking for the cold, hard facts—some real crisp information you can nosh on—get yourself a real guidebook. There are plenty out there with high-quality images of live birds—some real whackin' material. If you don't want facts, and what you desire is little cartoonish drawings of birds and wacky stories about what was going on when we saw them, you're in the right place. These are all the birds that we saw or heard in one year, roughly in that order.

I've had a Golden field guide (blue) of North American birds for as long as I can remember—probably a gift from my grandma. My grandma likes some birds, but you wouldn't call her a birder. She also doesn't like some birds, like the Brown-headed Cowbird. One spring, she found one of their eggs in a robin's nest on her porch and promptly took it out. Probably made breakfast with it—she's a great cook. I love my grandma. The field guide has always been around, and one fall day in 2023 I started flipping through the thing and thinking—*How ridiculous is it that there are this many birds?*—and—*Some of these have to be made up.*

After a spot of *research*, I found myself stoned to the bone in the backyard, staring up into a tree, using my last functioning neuron to decide if the bird I was looking at was a Downy Woodpecker or a Hairy Woodpecker. This was the first time I birded on purpose—other than the time my cousin and I killed five to six *"morning"* pigeons with an air rifle in Phoenix for no reason at all—and I do regret doing that.

Owen and I didn't know many birds before this, but we could name a few. We knew what a Northern Cardinal was—they're the mascot for the local baseball team. We could also tell you with near certainty whether a bird was a duck or a goose. To me, any little brownish-grey bird was called a Chickadee.

In late 2023, we became aware of a community of human beings that purposefully and continuously seeks to be in the proximity of specific birds. Some of them then go on to log the experience in a public database. An even smaller number of those people do this competitively, attempting to log the most bird encounters in the county, state, country, or even larger areas. The highest level of competition seems to be logging the most in a calendar year. They call it a *"big year,"* and they say it sort of quietly, a lot of them. Like it's kind of a secret that they're spending thousands of dollars to list different types of flying animals they've seen. We thought we should find out what's up with these folks—by becoming some of these folks. It turns out, this is an extremely passionate group.

Having successfully identified a bird in the field, the only logical next step was to do a big year. We are not bad at finding stuff. We've successfully found fossils and morel mushrooms, and I have a knack for finding ticks on my body, so we were pretty sure we could put up some serious numbers in the bird game our rookie year. It would also be a huge knowledge quest—jumping into the deep end, so to speak. What better way to learn about birds and birders than to seek out, observe, and film as many as we could?

Laying Down The Law

 The game is to observe as many different species of bird as you can within a calendar year (Jan 1st–Dec 31st). You can define your own boundaries if you want, but the most common and competitive areas are the ABA Area and the *Lower 48 United States*. We stuck to the Lower 48 to keep things simple. Some people do county, state, country, or even world big years, and people have added all sorts of modifiers—bicycle big years, blind big years, even naked big years. Our only modifier was that we wouldn't use any air travel, just driving—but you can make it whatever you want as long as you follow a few hard rules.

The ABA, or American Birding Association, has a set of recording rules they'd like you to abide by when maintaining any sort of list. You can view them by scanning the QR code. This is one of many QR codes in this book, and I promise they get less boring after this. Essentially, the rules state that in order to count a bird on your list, you must see or hear the bird within the boundaries of the United States, or up to 200 miles offshore. The rules also state that the bird must be alive, wild, and unrestrained. No problem.

Equipment & Logistics

Camera
The Nikon Coolpix P1000 is the only camera that exists on planet Earth as far as I'm concerned. If you want to take shi*tty—but still identifiable—images of birds that are a quarter mile away, look no further than one of humanity's greatest achievements. I purchased mine used on eBay for $650 USD. Not only would I be new to birdwatching, I'd be new to photography as well. Owen is a well-established wildlife and time-lapse photographer, but I would struggle to find the shutter button on a camera. The P1000 is a great entry-level camera. I could zoom to my heart's desire and make positive identifications in the field. I stuck to one mode for the entire year. Owen showed me a mode where I'd only

ever need to worry about changing the shutter speed—and, of course, dialing the focus ring, which did take some practice. The P1000 will not land you a Pulitzer Prize, but rather should be used as a scientific data collection tool. I was able to get data of ~90% of the birds.

Minivan

A used 2010 Kia Sedona (Base Model) minivan set me back $4,500 USD, but it proved to be the perfect vessel for this quest—and the best vehicle I've ever owned. During the course of the year, we put nearly 40,000 miles on it and gave it a life most other minivans could only dream of. We went through two full sets of tires—the cheapest ones they sell at Walmart. We did all the maintenance ourselves, which included oil changes, brakes, shocks, struts, and axles. The van had working heat and AC for the whole year.

Inside the van, we took out the back seats and installed military bunk-bed cots. This is where we would sleep almost every night. Occasionally, we would tent camp or sleep on someone's couch. We made all of our meals on a butane stove in the back of the van—I'll share some recipes later.

Ivy League Bird Software

No novice birdwatcher is fully equipped without their bird software. The software is a Cornell product. One component is for logging and exploring bird sightings in a public database—*eBird*. The other is for identifying birds—*Merlin*. eBird and his little brother Merlin are valuable tools that we relied on heavily throughout the year. They'll be referred to from here on out as the *"bird software."*

eBird 

 Merlin

Optics

We had one pair of broken boat binoculars to start with. We didn't use them at all, but we brought them with us. We just used our eyes and our cameras for the first three months. Our fortunes would change later on.

Planning

Most people who do this are extremely serious about it. They plan meticulously and know exactly where to position themselves throughout the year to see the most birds in the most efficient way—not to mention they usually have many years of experience under their belt, so they aren't seeing each bird for the first time. Our planning went like this: I Google-searched which states had the most birds. Florida, Texas, Arizona, California. We knew we'd find a lot of birds in those states, so that's where we'd go. The rest we'd figure out along the way.

How This Book Works

This book is broken up into sections, each one covering a trip we went on. At the beginning of each section, there's a map, some data, and an overview. Within each section, you'll find the bird plates and the text. The bird plates are my depictions of birds we saw or heard, in the way that we saw them. If we only saw the bird in its nonbreeding

plumage, that's how I drew it. *Plumage* refers to the outfit the bird is wearing. In general, birds wear their nonbreeding plumage in the winter, because they're not worried about getting laid. In the summer, they wear their breeding plumage to increase their chances of getting laid. For the most part, breeding males are the easiest to identify—they're the most *conspicuous*. That's French for *"it for sure is what it is."* If we only saw a female, or I think the female is cooler, then I drew a female. If we only heard it, it's depicted accordingly. If it's unlabeled, then the bird is an adult and the two sexes are indistinguishable. Otherwise, it's a bunch of hot breeding males. The left-hand page is where you'll find the text. Each bird depicted on the right-hand page corresponds to an entry on the left. Each entry includes the bird's name, a few symbols, and some information.

Labels and Symbols

m. = male
f. = female
im. = immature
j. = juvenile
br. = breeding
nb. = nonbreeding

Each bird is labeled according to the plumage it's depicted in.

= *very common*

= *common but localized*

= *rare, some breed here*

= *very rare*

= *super fu*ckin' rare*

= *extinct*

The dice symbols correspond to the bird's *rarity code*—a code assigned by the ABA that tells you how common or rare the bird is.

= *seen*

= *not seen*

= *heard*

= *not heard*

= *non-native*

The eye symbol is green if we saw the bird, and red if we didn't see the bird. The ear symbol is green if we heard it, and red if we didn't hear it. There's an asterisk symbol if the bird isn't native to the United States, but was introduced by humans and has since established a wild population. These birds are considered countable by the ABA.

On Bird Names:
The bird government voted to change the common names of many birds. Mostly birds that are named after humans. The names of the birds in this book were the names of the birds at the time we saw them. Soon they may be different.

Home Front

Duration: 4 days
Distance: 182mi
New Birds: 79
Total Birds: 79

Significant Places: Backyard, Bohm Woods Nature Preserve, Horseshoe Lake State Park, Riverlands Migratory Bird Sanctuary, Columbia Bottoms Conservation Area, MCT Bike Trails, Southern Illinois University-Edwardsville Campus.

Weather: Cold and grey.

Overview

The greater St. Louis area is home to plenty of birds for a couple of novices. Our home base is just over the river from the city, in Illinois. We decided we'd start easy and look for all the birds we could in the area. Scattered between the farm fields and suburbs, there are several great birding spots. We would get to know them well throughout the year. The weather was cold as fu*ck, and everything was grey—not exactly enticing birdwatching weather.

Even though the year had begun, the four days we spent around home felt like the preseason. We were just getting our touches in, going through the motions. Learning how to make a checklist on the bird software, getting experience taking a photo of a bird, organizing our scientific data—this sort of thing.

On the first day of the year, we added 62 species to our list. We were on fire. At this rate, they'd have to start making new species for us by midyear. Of course, we'd find out only a few weeks in that these were all the most common birds in the United States, and we'd see them again and again throughout the year. Nonetheless, we felt confident about our start.

Backyard Birds

European Starling 

The first bird of the year. Some Shakespeare-loving redcoat let a few loose in Central Park in the 1800s, and now they're everywhere. Beautiful bird, in the right light. You could call them successful at what they do.

Yellow-rumped Warbler 

Hardy warbler, ya gotta give em that.

American Goldfinch 

Never once had an issue with a Goldfinch. The male is bright yellow, the female is pretty drab—but hey, no worries.

Song Sparrow 

Sing us a song, you're the sparrow, man. Sing us a song to-night.

House Finch 

I'm gonna start crating up birds I think England should have, and sail my own ship across the Atlantic to deliver them.

Carolina Wren 

Song: *jeopardy-jeopardy-jeopardy. look at me, look at me, look at me. turkey meat, turkey meat, turkey meat. tickle feet, tickle feet, tickle feet.*

Northern Cardinal 

World Series Champs: 1926, 1931, 1934, 1942, 1944, 1946, 1964, 1967, 1982, 2006, 2011.

Blue Jay 

World Series Champs: 1992, 1993

American Robin

Heavy-set thrush. I'd need all my fingers and toes to count the times I've been anointed by these birds. Used to hate them, but in hindsight, I guess they're not so bad.

European Starling
Yellow-rumped Warbler
American Goldfinch
m.
f.
Song Sparrow
House Finch
f.
m.
Carolina Wren
Northern Cardinal
m.
f.
Blue Jay
American Robin
f.

Gang Activity

Even as a couple novices, we began to notice something about these six birds. It always seems like they were hanging out together, at least in our neck of the woods. If you saw one, you'd likely see the others.

Tufted Titmouse

Titmouse, Boobrat—ha ha, very fu*ckin' funny. Let's get it all out of the way now, because the rest of this book is very serious and full of scientific data. There's no time for these immature remarks. This bird has fantastic core strength.

Carolina Chickadee

Chickadees are just some of the boys.

White-breasted Nuthatch

Little trunk-dwelling tree clowns. I'd be lyin' if I said I didn't hatch a little nut every once in a while too.

Golden-crowned Kinglet

I got really pi*ssed on the second day of the year when I struggled to obtain an image of one of these tiny little pee boners. This would be a regular occurrence moving forward. No one talks enough about how difficult it is to capture a nice image of a bird that's only a couple inches long and never stops moving.

Ruby-crowned Kinglet

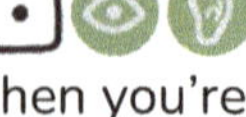

Also known as a *Rub-me-down* Kinglet, because when you're new to birdwatching, you get caught up on the names. A lot of them are ridiculous, and it's low-hanging fruit—easy pickins for a couple greaseballs like us. You're gonna like this bird when it's angry. The male only shows his ruby crown when agitated.

Brown Creeper

Owen says he had a buddy in high school that he used to call the same name. These camouflaged birds dwell on trunks like nuthatches do, but only travel upward—whereas nuthatches will go both ways.

Tufted
Titmouse
Carolina
Chickadee
f.
White-breasted
Nuthatch
Golden-crowned
Kinglet
m.
Ruby-crowned
Kinglet
m.
showing
ruby
f.
Brown
Creeper

Peckerwoods

Woodpeckers are trunk tappers. They zip around trees, and look for stuff to eat. They are pre-programmed to search for grubs and bugs, and whatnot inside of and around trees. Most of the woodpeckers we saw throughout the year had four toes on each foot. Some woodpeckers only have three—but we'll get there later.

Hairy Woodpecker 

Has no hair on it at all—believe me. Compared to the Downy Woodpecker, the Hairy Woodpecker is generally more robust. It also has a *larger* bill-size-to-head-size ratio. They say it's one of the first ID challenges a new birdwatcher encounters.

Downy Woodpecker 

Just a smaller woodpecker in general than the Hairy Wood-pecker. Downy Woodpeckers also have a *smaller* bill-size-to-head-size ratio. The male has a little red on the back of his head. The female does not. This seems to be the case with a lot of woodpeckers. The male might have a smidge more red somewhere on the head or face.

Red-bellied Woodpecker 

I don't like these woodpeckers, I just don't. They seem like a scam. See: Golden-fronted & Gila Woodpecker.

Northern Flicker 

Flickers will be on the ground a lot of times, actually—down there flicking, I guess.

Red-headed Woodpecker 

The head is red, just like it says. The head is red, just like it says.

Pileated Woodpecker 

Large woodpecker. It's superficially similar to the Ivory-billed Woodpecker, but they say the Ivory-billed is likely extinct. Some folks pronounce it *"pill-ee-ated,"* while others say *"pie-lee-ated."* One of those groups stood too close to a microwave when they were kids. See: Ivory-billed Woodpecker.

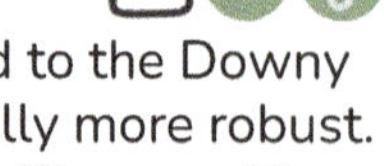

Hairy Woodpecker
f.
Red-bellied Woodpecker
f.
m.
m.
Downy Woodpecker
f.
Northern Flicker
m.
Red-headed Woodpecker
f.
Pileated Woodpecker

Birds of Wire

Birdwatching while driving set in pretty early on for me. It's a precursor to chronic birdwatching, and you've just gotta keep an eye on it—keep an eye on the road.

Northern Mockingbird  

Never mad about seeing one of these, really. Not even the time we stopped traffic for a minute on a two-lane highway because I thought I saw a super rare bird—it was a mocking-bird. Pretty embarrassing. The Northern Mockingbird mimics sounds it hears just like me and Owen.

American Kestrel  

Little falcon, kinda painted up like it works at the circus.

House Sparrow   

Home Depot. Can't miss 'em.

Eurasian Tree Sparrow   

They were introduced in St. Louis in 1870, the same place where we were introduced over a hundred years later. The males are very similar to a male House Sparrow but with a clear and distinct cheek spot. It's all about the cheek spot. In my experience, they hang out slightly farther from human development than the House Sparrow—so they might not nest at The Home Depot, but they're close enough in case they need to make a repair.

Eastern Bluebird   

Old ladies fu*cking love bluebirds.

Rock Pigeon  

If there *is* a bird that serves as a surveillance device, obviously this one would be ideal. They come in several different finishes.

Mourning Doves  

They ain't botherin' nobody. Our buddy Mason does a great impression of them. Song: *coowuh-cooo-oo-oo*

Northern Mockingbird
American Kestrel
f.
vole
House Sparrow
Eurasian Tree Sparrow
m.
m.
f.
Eastern Bluebird
Rock Pigeon
Mourning Dove

Entry-Level Sparrows

American Tree Sparrow

Breast spot, right in the middle. Top of the bill is dark. Has a rusty cap and eyepiece. *Rusty* is another way to say *brown* when describing bird plumage—if they just used *brown* all the time, things would get boring.

Field Sparrow

Beautiful descending song. One of those birds you'd rather hear than see.

White-throated Sparrow

Plump little whistlers, fat little bells.

White-crowned Sparrow

At a quick glance, they look very similar to the White-throated Sparrow. However, the White-crowned Sparrow is more slender, and alien-like.

Fox Sparrow

Never saw its face, and never saw it again. We heard the bird well, but it was hidden in the bushes. We got a quick glimpse of the reddish-brown bird, obscured by sticks. We would never lay eyes on one again during the year—just one brief encounter. That's all you need, according to the rules. The rules don't state that you must observe the bird for a certain amount of time—just that you see it or hear it, while it's alive and unrestrained.

Dark-eyed Junco

A dark grey sparrow with a little pink bill. They make a tinkly, chipping noise and seem to spend a lot of time on the ground. Easily identified with a quick glance. Look for the white tail feathers flashing as they fly away.

Eastern Towhee

Towhee is French for *"large sparrow that kicks leaves and dirt around."* The male is black, the female is brown.
Song: *sex-for—free-e-e-e-e*

American
Tree
Sparrow
Field
Sparrow
White-crowned
Sparrow
White-throated
Sparrow
tail
Dark-eyed
Junco
f.
m.
Fox Sparrow
Eastern
Towhee
m.
f.

Meatlovers

Turkey Vulture

Turkey Vultures, or *TVs* for short, are large black scavengers. They soar high in the sky with their wings held in a shallow V shape as they look—and smell—for dead animals below.

Bald Eagle

It's on all the money, and they bring one into your school sometimes when you're a little kid. Then there's a firefighter there for some reason, and you have to start chanting something about a flag while they're telling you, *"Yeah, we **are** the good guys!"*

Red-tailed Hawk

Large and ubiquitous.

Red-shouldered Hawk

 This is one of the birds we got to see in the act of mating. The cloacal kiss is a magical thing, and nothing can prepare you for it.

Great Horned Owl

Big, beefy hooters that'll keep you up at night.

Sharp-shinned Hawk

Quiet, agile, little murderer of the woods. If you report one of these on the bird software, you'll most likely get an email back from a local mouth-breather telling you that what you saw was not what you saw. Difficult to distinguish from the more common Cooper's Hawk. In flight, note the Sharp-shinned Hawk's flat tail tip and lack of neck.

Cooper's Hawk

Most of the time, when you see a smaller hawk with a long tail, it'll end up being a Cooper's Hawk. They're usually larger than the Sharp-shinned Hawk, but pay attention to other field marks if you can—or even want to. The Cooper's Hawk has a more rounded tail tip, a blockier, flatter head, and a longer neck.

Turkey Vulture
detailed head view
Bald Eagle
Red-tailed Hawk
Red-shouldered Hawk
Great Horned Owl
flight profiles
Cooper's Hawk
Sharp-shinned Hawk

Cold Field

Northern Harrier

Named after the VTOL military aircraft

Short-eared Owl

A daytime owl—if you believe in all that.

American Crow

They surely smoke cigarettes when we aren't looking. They've got a certain confidence about them—like the whole bird thing is a cakewalk.

Horned Lark

Can be very difficult to see out there. They blend in well, but a good look at this bird is a pleasure. Real sharp bird. Dressed to impress, but it's not too cocky.

Killdeer

Killdeer make nests on the ground. In the spring, we found one in the gravel parking lot of a local nature preserve. We'd check in on it every so often. It seemed like it could easily get scrambled by a tire, so one day I stole some little orange and pink utility flags from someone's yard and stuck them around it—just like I'd seen them do at the Audubon Center. Every few days or so, we'd come back to check, and all was well. The lot started getting a bit overgrown with grass, and about three weeks from the day we first found the nest, we went to check again, thinking they must've hatched by now. What we found was just terrible. Someone had mowed over the area and scrambled the nest.

"This is right up there with 9/11."
—Owen

Northern Harrier
Short-eared Owl
American Crow
Horned Lark
Killdeer
nest

Local Marsh

Many a bird was found in a marsh.

Red-winged Blackbird

Ubiquitous. Female is underrated.

Belted Kingbird

Fishing specialist. These birds dive into water to hunt fish. Bigger than most perching birds, but smaller than most of the killing birds. It has the bill of a heron but the hunting style of a bird of prey. In this case, the female has the more appealing plumage, wearing a reddish piece on the chest and sides. Call is a high-pitched rattle that echoes across the water.

Swamp Sparrow

Kinda like a dirtier, stinkier Song Sparrow. See: Song Sparrow.

Marsh Wren

This is a secretive marsh bird. It prefers to stay well hidden in the cattails. Shortly after finding one at the local marsh, we watched a man stumble out of a weedy field at sunset, about 200 yards away. He had a beer in his hand and his a*ss on full display. I sniped this image of him with the P1000. Just another day at Horseshoe Lake, really.

American Coot

Common marsh resident. An all-black, duck-like bird with a white beak. It's not a duck, but it kinda swims like a duck does. As a novice, you'd assume it's a type of duck—but take one look at the feet and you'll change your tune. Later in the year, we saw a mother with babies. The baby American Coot might be one of the ugliest creatures on the face of the Earth, but just understand—it's not finished. It's still under construction.

Pied-billed Grebe

Grebes dive to hunt for fish. It can be entertaining to watch them disappear and try to guess where they'll pop back up. This particular grebe is small, but not the smallest one they make. Look for the black band around its bill.

f.
Red-winged
Blackbird
m.
Belted
Kingfisher
f.
Swamp
Sparrow
Marsh Wren
Pied-billed
Grebe
American
Coot
chick

Drakes in Lakes

Ducks are boring. I'll be the first to say it. Some of them are beautiful, strikingly patterned creatures—but I don't love ducks. It's as simple as that. I used to work at a Chinese restaurant, and one of my jobs was to take a frozen duck from the freezer, microwave it for 10 minutes, flip it, then do another 10. I think that could have something to do with it. That said, ducks are important—and so is duck hunting. It might sound counterintuitive, but killing ducks (legally) directly supports the conservation of the habitat they—and many other species—depend on. I was gifted a *duck stamp*, a $25 permit required by the U.S. Fish and Wildlife Service to hunt migratory waterfowl in the United States. I thought it was so cool that I bought another one, even though I didn't have any plans to kill a duck. You should think about buying one yourself. Just know you can't use it as postage. Believe me—I tried.

Mallard

Pronounced *"muh-lahrd."* This is your meat-and-potatoes duck.

Gadwall

Just a slate-grey-brown duck out there. Kinda flat, kinda long. Looks to be hardy.

Ruddy Duck

Small duck. Tail's all cocked up.

Redhead

Males have a red head and could possibly be confused with a Canvasback at a distance. See: Canvasback.

Bufflehead

Small duck, pleasing to the eye.

Common Goldeneye

Holy smokes, I just wanna swim out there after it.

Northern Shoveler

Huge, shovel-like bill is conspicuous.

males
Mallard
Gadwall
Ruddy
Duck
Redhead
Common
Goldeneye
Bufflehead
Northern
Shoveler

These Are Also Ducks

Lesser Scaup

Greater Scaup

These two ducks look very similar. They both have black front halves and a lighter greyish back half. They both have a grey bill, and a yellow eye. To tell them apart, look for a little hairdo. If the duck looks like it has a subtle hairdo in the back, then it's most likely a Lesser Scaup. The Greater Scaup has no hairdo. It's head is very round.

Ring-necked Duck

It's gonna be a *ringed-neck* duck when I'm done with it. This duck is much like the previous two, but you can see some bold white edging around the bill—like it just drank a glass of milk.

Hooded Merganser

Quirky duck. When aroused, the male puffs up its white head-piece. *Mergansing* isn't an action, it's more like a state of mind.

Red-breasted Merganser

The male has an orange bill and a dark green hairdo. It has a red eye, a white collar and some other features as well. The female also has an orange bill. It has a brownish-orange hairdo and a grey body. Half of birdwatching is just playing that game where you find the differences between two similar images.

Common Merganser

Clinically patterned duck. Male has a reddish orange bill with a dark tip. It has a dark green head and a mostly white body. The female looks very similar to the female Red-breasted Merganser, however, it has a white throat. Can be hard to see at a distance.

"Yeah, no, for sure. I definitely see how you could say that one has a little hairdo. Yeah, yeah, I saw it."
—Owen

Greater
Scaup
Lesser
Scaup
Ring-necked
Duck
males
Hooded
Merganser
horny
m.
f.
Red-breasted
Merganser
m.
f.
Common
Merganser
m.
f.

Trailer Park Pond

There's a dinky trailer park pond in town that provides some entertaining wildlife viewing opportunities. It's best to keep your head on a swivel while you're there. Practice the buddy system.

Ring-billed Gull

 Adult Ring-billed Gulls have a black ring painted around their otherwise yellow bill. They have grey wings and black wingtips like a lot of seagulls. They'll try to eat anything they can get their beaks on—whatever size or shape—even the material doesn't seem to matter.

Herring Gull

A well-read Herring might've known better than to land here. Everybody's watching that Ring-bill choke on the fish for the fourth time, but no one's asking why that shovel has blood on it.

Bonaparte's Gull

It's gonna be a *blown-apart* gull when I'm done with it.

American Wigeon

Thank God it's an American Wigeon and not a British or a French Wigeon.

Black-bellied Whistling Duck

This bird was rare for the area. They aren't rare in the United States by any means, but they aren't usually found in Illinois. This is an important distinction to make. Rarity is all relative.

"I can't tell if that guy's fishing over there or disposing of a dead body."
—Owen

Ring-billed Gull
Herring Gull
nb.
Bonaparte's Gull
nb.
human remains probably
American Wigeon
Black-bellied Whistling Duck

Gooses & Swans

Canada Goose

If they're so Canadian, why don't they stay up there?

Cackling Goose

When Canada Geese talk to Cackling Geese, they say things like *"Hey buddy"* and *"What's up big guy!"* We spent 2-3 hours in sub freezing temperatures sorting through thousands of Canada Geese to find this smaller proportioned look-a-like.

Greater White-fronted Goose

A year ago, I didn't know there were more types of geese than the Canada Goose. When I saw these for the first time, I thought—*Okay, that's enough.*

Snow Goose

One day we saw a Snow Goose split off from its flock mid-air to join a group of soaring pelicans. The next day we saw it again, still flying with the pelicans. It is a pelican now.
See: American White Pelican.

Ross's Goose

The Ross's Goose is to the Snow Goose as the Cackling Goose is to the Canada Goose.

Trumpeter Swan

We saw several orchestras flying overhead on the first day of the year. Possibly more closely related to tubas than trumpets, they are massive.

Mute Swan

I've never heard one make any noise, so yeah, I believe it.

Tundra Swan

Like a Trumpeter Swan, but not quite as musically inclined.

Canada
Goose
Canada
Goose
Cackling
Goose
(agitated)
Greater
White-fronted
Goose
Ross's
Goose
Snow
Goose
Trumpeter Swan
Mute
Swan
Tundra
Swan

First Florida

January

Duration: 20 days
Distance: 2,738mi
New Birds: 109
Total Birds: 188
Cracker Barrel Stays: 12

General Route: South through Birmingham, to Dauphin Island. Across and down the gulf coast. Inland to Homestead, up through Miami to Merrit Island. Back west to Ocala.

Significant Places: Wheeler NWR, Dauphin Island, St. Marks NWR, Cedar Key, J.N. Ding Darling NWR, The Celery Fields, Frog Pond, Homestead, Miami, Merritt Island, Ocala, Longleaf Pine Forests.

Weather: Cloudy and rainy. We were caught in several a*ss-puckering storms. We did not see the sun a whole lot. Overall it was an uncomfortable time.

Overview

We ate the worst meal of the entire year on our first night out, at a lake near Cairo, Illinois—an abandoned town at the southern tip of the state. We'd bought *steak bites*, little cubes of cow meat on sale at the grocery store. I cooked them on the two-burner Coleman in the back of the minivan. We ate the bland, grey tendon balls in the dark at 4:30 p.m., then just laid down for sixteen hours. The rest of the trip was about as tough as those sorry cubes of flesh.

Florida doesn't have much easily accessible public land compared to the western states. We found as much free camping on public land as we could, but it was often far from the birds we were after. When there wasn't a decent outdoor spot nearby, we could usually count on a Cracker Barrel Old Country Store. They let you *overnight park* for free. You don't even have to eat the food—and you shouldn't. It's bad for you. We'll always be grateful for Cracker Barrel's parking policies. Over the course of the year, we spent a total of 42 nights in their lots across the country, but none more than in the state of Florida.

We were true novices. We didn't even know how to use the bird software correctly yet. We were unaware of a feature that filters for birds not yet on your list. Instead, we'd scroll around the maps until we found a report for a bird we thought we hadn't seen, or we'd Google where to find certain birds we saw in the big guidebook we lugged around.

Finding birds was one thing—identifying them was a whole different ball game. We'd take tons of photos of any bird that looked slightly different, then try to ID it later in the van. This was how we learned, and it was a slow, grinding process. Later in the year, when we were much better birders, we realized we probably could've spent five days in Florida instead of twenty, and seen just as many new birds.

As tough as it was, this was our purest trip. Just two guys bein' dudes—birdwatching by day, sleepin' in a minivan together by night.

Blackbrown Catcow

Grey Catbird   

Their whining can get on your nerves at times, but these birds make a variety of entertaining imitations.

Brown-headed Cowbird  

 The epitome of working smart, not hard. These birds don't build their own nests or raise their own young. Instead, the female lays her egg in another bird's nest, and that bird raises it for her.

Boat-tailed Grackle  

Large and loud blackbird, they dominate the coast. Males are black with a huge tail and a purple sheen in the right light; females are brown. In coastal Texas, they overlap slightly with the Great-tailed Grackle but are less likely to be found at a gas station. See: Great-tailed Grackle.

Brown Thrasher   

The only reason I'd ever heard of a *thrasher* was because of the former NHL team, the Atlanta Thrashers (RIP). The Brown Thrasher is the only thrasher native to the Atlanta area, so that must have been what the team was based on. It's kind of a shy, secretive bird—not especially intimidating. Maybe that's why the franchise moved.

Fish Crow   

Best distinguished from the American Crow by voice—or by holding it underwater for five minutes. If it's still moving when you pull it back up, it's a Fish Crow.

Common Grackle   

Base model. If you want the fancy tail, it's gonna cost a little extra.

Rusty Blackbird   

They can get so rusty they just turn white. One of the birds we saw was *leucistic*—some sort of bird STD.

Grey
Catbird
Brown-headed
Cowbird
m.
f.
egg
Boat-tailed
Grackle
f.
m.
Brown
Thrasher
Fish Crow
Common
Grackle
Rusty
Blackbird

Herons

Green Heron

Owen went prone next to a pond with alligators in it to film this little heron fishing, while I jumped on a small trampoline someone had dumped nearby.

Yellow-crowned Night Heron

Saw this one on Sanibel Island. If all goes well, I'll never set foot on that island again. It was the only new bird we saw while we were there, and we'd go on to see them many more times elsewhere. We got stuck on the island for nearly four hours on a Saturday evening—there's only one road in and out of that godforsaken place.

Black-crowned Night Heron

In our experience they really do get a little more rowdy after the sun goes down. They kept waking us up one night when we boondocked at a fishing pier.

Little Blue Heron

Not the greatest blue heron, but runs and operates as it should. Softer, quieter, smaller, and less intimidating than other blue herons.

Tricolored Heron

I'll let ya in on a little secret—it's got more than three colors.

Great Blue Heron

You'll want to avoid being a small animal of any kind near one of these birds. To us humans, this is a large, majestic wading bird. To anything small near water, it's what nightmares are made of. The Great Blue Heron is an iconic bird and a great bridge between birders and civilians. It seems like everyone has seen one. They're everywhere, and large enough that regular people notice them. A fantastic introductory bird—and an absolute weapon.

Yellow-crowned
Night Heron
Green
Heron
Black-crowned
Night Heron
Little
Blue
Heron
Great
Blue
Heron
Tricolored
Heron

Egrets & Ibises

Glossy Ibis

A sort of glossy finish, if you catch it in the right light. Plumage coloration is that of mint-raspberry dark chocolate. Compare to the similar White-faced Ibis. See: White-faced Ibis

White Ibis

It's called an *ibi fly-by* when a group of them flies past. In Florida, it's not uncommon to see these birds perched on light poles or electrical wires. It doesn't look right—like they don't belong up there—but Florida's a wild place.

Western Cattle Egret

Small white fishing bird that's more of a fan of dry land than the other fishing birds. You'll likely see one in a patch of grass or a farm field—fishing for bugs. For some reason they don't like water as much as their other egret brethren.

Snowy Egret

Medium-sized white fishing bird. Look for the bright yellow feet. I love Tabasco hot sauce because the family that created it is credited with almost single-handedly saving these birds after the species got all banged up from the plume trade. The plume trade was a market where dudes would go out and shoot birds for their feathers, then make ridiculous hats out of them to sell to their musty girlfriends. I read that in a book—and now you did too.

Great Egret

I'm not qualified to tell you if it's a great egret, or even a good one. What I *can* tell you is that this is the largest egret our team was able to locate. A large white fishing bird with a crooked-a*ss neck.

Reddish Egret

Large fishing bird that takes a more active approach. Does not rely on a slow methodical sneak attack. These birds prefer a more thrilling chase.

Glossy
Ibis
White
Ibis
Western
Cattle
Egret
nb.
Snowy
Egret
Great
Egret
SCABATO
hot
sauce
Reddish
Egret
fish

Weird Fishermen

Wood Stork

When we saw this bird, it of course became the reigning champion for ugliest bird of the year—but it was later dethroned by a baby American Coot. See: American Coot.

Roseate Spoonbill

A bird with a built-in utensil. The male has a spoon-shaped bill, so naturally the female has a fork-shaped bill. These birds are not flamingos. If you think it's a flamingo, you're really not paying attention to detail. See: American Flamingo.

Sandhill Crane

Very tall grey bird with a red mask. Often in large groups. Could be considered gang activity. Their calls are like Jurassic Park.

Anhinga

Anhingas are known colloquially as the *snake bird* because of their long, snakey neck. They dive underwater to catch fish. One time, we watched one dive down and come back up with a decent-sized catfish skewered on its bill. It proceeded to beat the wheels off the fish and swallow it whole.

Limpkin

The Limpkin used to be limpin', but now it's thriving. The spread of the non-native Apple Snail in the Southeast has been a huge benefit for them. Limpkins fu*cking love snails.

American Bittern

Found this bird in a roadside ditch. We were walking by and saw some movement on the side of the road—a decent-sized animal had backed into the grass just out of view. We came back in the van, parked at the spot, and waited. Sure enough, a few minutes later, this strange bird poked its neck out. It's funny how birds are scared of bipedal primates, but a two-ton hunk of metal is no factor.

Wood
Stork
Roseate
Spoonbill
f.
m.
Sandhill
Crane
Anhinga
with
prey
item
day
dream
Limpkin
American
Bittern

As Far As We Could Sea

Our optics at the time were the Nikon P1000 and one pair of broken *"boat"* binoculars. We were told there were many birds farther out in the ocean—but we wouldn't be able to see or identify them yet. Luckily, there are plenty of birds near the beach.

American White Pelican

Huge white bird. Gargantuous deep throater. You'll want to observe them soaring together in a large flock—it's a quite a sight.

Brown Pelican

 At a wildlife rehabilitation center we watched a woman, who was blind in one eye, snatch the bill of a Brown Pelican, straddle it, and then shove her arm down its throat to deliver a dose of medicine. Later in the year, we saw some of these birds overheat. When they do that, they puke their spines out of their mouth. I generally feel uneasy about the Brown Pelican.

Surf Scoter

Clowny sea duck

American Oystercatcher

Catching an oyster is not that impressive, but shucking an oyster with just your face? Now that's something to write home about. We saw this bird while on the Dauphin Island ferry. A ferry ride is a reasonable amount of time at sea.

Double-crested Cormorant

Default Cormorant. Cormorants swim not entirely unlike ducks—but set a little lower in the water. Most of their body stays submerged at the surface, with just the neck sticking out. Then they dive underwater and catch fish. How terrifying that must be for a fish.

Laughing Gull

They do laugh, and a lot of times it seems to be at you.

American White Pelican
Brown
Pelican
spine
Surf Scoter
m.
Double-crested
Cormorant
Ha
ha!
Laughing
Gull
American
Oystercatcher
nb.
!
oyster

Owen's Tern

Owen wasn't as concerned as I was with finding as many new birds as we could in the beginning. He was more focused on getting a good video of a bird's behavior—or a video of me pi*ssed off that I couldn't find a new bird. He studied the text less than I did, and overall, he wasn't as good at finding birds as I was. He just wasn't as into it—that wasn't his job. That was my job. That said, he'd still come through big on occasion. He'd come out of left field and point out a new bird that was right in front of me. Sometimes you could show him a picture of a bird, and he'd smell it like a hound dog—you'd follow him around for a while until he stopped and pointed right at it. He was also an absolute weapon with the bird software. You could ask him what was making that noise, and before you could even finish, he'd be rattling off the possibilities.

Royal Tern

 The subject of one of our early lab sessions. This large tern is similar to the Caspian Tern, however, the Royal Tern's bill is more orange than red. It also has a flatter-topped head.

Caspian Tern

A large tern. Bill is a bit more red than that of the Royal Tern.

Sandwich Tern

We walked onto the beach, and within 20 seconds Owen pointed at a bird and said with utmost confidence and matter-of-factness, *"That's a Sandwich Tern,"* as if he had seen a thousand of them. I'd never heard of this bird yet. This was the first of Owen's big finds.

Common Tern

It's actually the tern we saw the least amount of times.

Forster's Tern

Small tern, but not the smallest. Long, deeply forked tail.

Black Skimmer

Like a big pair of scissors out there. None of that *safety* bullshi*t.

Royal
Tern
nb.
Caspian
Tern
nb.
tail
in flight
Common
Tern
nb.
Forster's
Tern
im.
Sandwich
Tern
nb.
skimming
nb.
Black Skimmer

Not So Shore Birds

Identification had been difficult, but manageable up to this point. For the birds we weren't sure about, we relied heavily on the Ivy League bird software. We were able to get decent photographs and audio recordings to aid in our dilemmas. Shorebirds were a different story. They're far away, and they're all the same color in the winter. You're looking for subtle differences in shape and size, for the most part. You can separate them all by voice, but the problem becomes—*which one made that little peep?* They might be in a mixed flock of several hundred birds or more at times. Certainly a time of major growth in our young career.

Dunlin

Kind of a sad, dumpy name for a bird that you could also describe as sad and dumpy. I think it might be the down-ward-curved bill that does it.

Red Knot

When I go on a cold, windy bike ride, I get a little red knot too—if you know what I mean. As far as the bird goes, it's plump and rotund with a stock, factory-issue bill—nothin' fancy. In nonbreeding plumage, it's greyish-brown, just like all the rest of them.

Long-billed Dowitcher

Short-billed Dowitcher

Short bill, long bill—who gives a shi*t? The real question is: what the he*ck is *Dowitching*?

Lesser Yellowlegs

Greater Yellowlegs

If you see them side by side, it's easy—smaller is Lesser, big-ger is Greater. Don't take a brain mechanic to figure that out. In reality, it doesn't always go that way. Size is hard to judge at a distance, and wildlife refuges don't just put yardsticks out in the muck for you. You're better off comparing proportions.

Willet

I don't know, it might.

Dunlin
nb.
Red Knot
nb.
Long-billed Dowitcher
nb.
Short-billed Dowitcher
nb.
Greater Yellowlegs
nb.
Lesser Yellowlegs
Willet
nb.

For Shore Birds

Semipalmated Plover

This bird is not *quite* all-the-way palmated.

Black-bellied Plover

Based on our field observations, plovers may be stuck in some sort of mentally handicapped purgatory. They seem to run for a second, then stop and look around. While paused, they go into an existential spiral—*What is all this? ... Where am I? ... Who am I? ... Why is...* And just as they start to get some-where, they snap out of it and start running again.

Sanderling

The foot speed alone should be enough to get a couple of looks from big league scouts.

Ruddy Turnstone

Go up to a stranger and tell them you saw a *Ruddy Turn-stone*—see how it goes.

Least Sandpiper

Not the last sandpiper of the year, but certainly the least. Small and greyish-brown, the Least Sandpiper is an unim-pressive little shorebird—and we love it for that reason.

Western Sandpiper

If you're looking for something a bit *more* than the Least Sandpiper, try one of these out.

Spotted Sandpiper

 If you only have time to see one sandpiper, make it this one. They consistently bounce their rear ends up and down ever so smoothly. It's not even a mating display—they just seem to do it to maintain homeostasis.

Semipalmated Plover
Black-bellied Plover
nb.
nb.
Ruddy Turnstone
Sanderling
nb.
nb.
Western Sandpiper
Least Sandpiper
nb.
nb.
Spotted Sandpiper
br.
bounce

Meatlovers

White-tailed Kite

They mostly eat bugs, but bugs is meat too. We walked about four miles south on a long black road at a place called Frog Pond, thinking we'd find something crazy out there. All that's out there is an old creepy rocket factory and a few dead snakes. We got caught in the rain with our cameras and had to run the four miles back to the parking lot, where we met a pro birder. He pointed one out to us—had it on a string.

Black Vulture

There are billboards in some parts of the country advertising solutions to Black Vulture problems on farms. I can't imagine the solutions end too well for the birds.

Short-tailed Hawk

Saw what we determined to be a *dark morph* of this species. Now we had to consider *morphs* and *juveniles* when identifying hawks for the first time. This whole thing was getting to be a bit involved.

Crested Caracara

Bird so nice, they named it twice.

Osprey

Named after the backpack company. Highly successful fish hunters. You wouldn't say they fish like a heron or an egret does—they hunt fish, they don't fish for them. Star of the show in Cedar Key. If you haven't been to Cedar Key, that's just fine—don't lose sleep over it.

Merlin

Named after the Ivy League bird software, this bird is comparable to the American Kestrel but not nearly as nicely patterned. Owen found one in a tree at a busy park—it was the only one we saw all year. See: American Kestrel.

White-tailed Kite
kiting
Black Vulture
dark morph
Short-tailed Hawk
Osprey
Crested Caracara
fish
Merlin

Flycatchers et al.

Great Crested Flycatcher

You can see them for free in the *********************** parking lot. We showed up to *********************** excited and hopeful for all the birds we might see, but we turned right around when we saw that admission was seventeen U.S. dollars. Holy smokes, bud—two of those is a tank of gas. We made a short video of ourselves dogging on the high prices while birdwatching in the parking lot instead. We put it on the internet and most people thought it was funny, while others were fuming. One person kept persisting—comments, messages, even emails. They referred to themselves as *"Skip Wiley."* Skip Wiley is a fictional character from an old novel about the leader of an eco-terrorist group that kills tourists and commits other acts of violence to scare people away and protect Florida's natural landscape. We believe this was the director of *********************** and that it was meant to be a threat. I hope they're doing well. I know they are, actually— they make a lot of money.

Loggerhead Shrike

Psychopathic murderer in a grey-and-black songbird's body.

White-eyed Vireo

The song is a dripping-wet, buzzy, metallic rap. They're very responsive to pishing—a highly pishable species. **Pishing** is when you make that sound with your mouth: *pshh pshh psshhh*. It's a totally acceptable way to try to call in a bird. There's no controversy to it—just don't go pishin' your pants.

Eastern Phoebe

Wags the tail. Flicks it down quickly, and then back up a little more slowly.

Vermilion Flycatcher

These are small but sturdy-bodied flycatchers. The male is bright red below and up top, with dark wings and mask. The female has a tasteful bit of salmon underneath and is brown on the top side. They're kind of uncommon in Florida—more of a Southwest bird.

Great Crested
Flycatcher
Loggerhead
Shrike
White-eyed
Vireo
Eastern
Phoebe
tail wag
m.
Vermilion
Flycatcher
f.

Birds On The Ground

Savannah Sparrow

Short-tailed sparrow. Clean. Real Clean. A little bit of yellow over the eye. Not too bad.

Grasshopper Sparrow

They are named this way because they are this way.

Eastern Meadowlark

The song will make you want to walk out into the meadow, fully naked, and frolic in the sunshine and flowers. I don't recommend acting on this feeling—just take a deep breath and let it pass. Compare to the Western and Chihuahuan Meadowlarks. They can all be told apart by voice, or by how many white tail feathers they have. The Eastern Meadowlark has three mostly white outer tail feathers, as does the Western. The Chihuahuan Meadowlark on the other hand has four mostly white outer tail feathers.

Wild Turkey

They put bread in its a*ss. Can you believe that?

Common Ground Dove

You'll see them on the ground, but don't assume they're limited to it. They can fly. Not flightless by any means. We saw one for the first time at a campground in Cedar Key. This campground had a very moldy shower, but it still got the job done. You take a shower when you can get one. Don't pass it up—you don't know when your next one's gonna be.

Burrowing Owl

 There's a sports park in the northern Miami area where they've roped off the burrows of these owls—like they're VIPs. These birds seem a little spazzy, like the kids at school who used to run to class without using their arms.

Savannah Sparrow
Grasshopper Sparrow
Eastern Meadowlark
tail
1
2
3
not to scale
Wild Turkey
Burrowing Owl
Common Ground Dove

Exotic Naturals Near Us

Florida is home to a lot of *introduced* wildlife. Many non-native birds are countable on a big year list. These are a few we were able to pick up.

Eurasian Collared Dove 

Light grey dove, noticeably larger than a Mourning Dove. Sports a dark collar on the back of the neck. Saw one for the first time in a Winn-Dixie parking lot. We stopped to stock up on taco supplies and use the bathroom. The toilet had a wooden seat, and I've always felt weird about places like that. We sat in the van for a while and did computer tasks—Owen was offloading and logging footage, while I was doing tasks for my job, which at the time was programming and managing bitcoin miners remotely. You'll see why this is relevant soon enough. See: Mourning Dove.

Common Myna 

Right across the street from the boiled peanut place is where we saw the first one. Boiled peanuts are pretty good—they weren't lyin'.

Nanday Parakeet 

Monk Parakeet 

There's a substation in St. Petersburg where dozens of parakeets roost and nest. They're very loud—and so is the surrounding area. This is where we realized that some birds wouldn't make it onto our list due to their proximity to major human development. Some non-native species are countable, but they're only found deep in cities. That wasn't our cup of tea. We'd rather search for a bird deep in the woods, and avoid all the madness. Florida was tough for this reason—the places with the most people also have the most birds.

Muscovy Duck 

Disgusting wart-covered bird. Very large for a duck. I wouldn't eat one if I was starving to death.

Egyptian Goose 

They know how and *why* it was done.

Eurasian Collared Dove
Common Myna
Nanday Parakeet
Monk Parakeet
eight trillion volts
power generator
Egyptian Goose
Muscovy Duck

More Ducks

If you thought we were done with ducks, you'd be wrong. The ducks in this field guide go all the way to the end—I promise you that.

Canvasback

Could be confused with a Redhead at a distance. See: Redhead.

Mottled Duck

When something is *mottled*, it means it's marked with splotches or smudges. For example, Owen mottled up the floor of the minivan when he spilled a full can of beans in there.

Green-winged Teal

The male is dressed up with a reddish-brown head and a green eye mask. The female—like nearly all the female ducks—is mostly brown and unassuming.

Blue-winged Teal

Based on our field observations, this duck is a small duck.

Northern Pintail

They say ducks can be pretty rapey, but the way Owen was speaking when he saw this one had me a little worried for the bird's safety.

Horned Grebe

Small grebe. Very similar to the Eared Grebe when both are in nonbreeding plumage. We didn't get to see this one in its breeding plumage—and that's okay, I wasn't dressed to the nines either. See: Eared Grebe.

Common Loon

Our mom always teased us about ending up in the loony bin. I'm starting to think we're already there.

"You can't just go out swimmin' around lookin' like that and expect everything to just go your way."
—Owen

Canvasback
Mottled Duck
Green-winged Teal
Blue-winged Teal
Northern Pintail
Horned Grebe
nb.
Common Loon

Winter Warblers

Yellow-throated Warbler

Small, active bird with a pointy bill. Grey above, and white below. Bright yellow throat and a black eye mask. Wing shows black wing bar, sandwiched by two white wing bars. Bold black streaks extend down the sides of the body. Subtle grey edging on the underside of the tail feathers. Sexes are similar. That is how a real guidebook would describe the appearance of a bird.

Yellow Warbler

This one's easy—it's all yellow.

American Redstart

Start me up. Start me up, I'll never stop.

Black-and-white Warbler

They are like nuthatches in that they prefer to dwell trunk rather than branch out.

Palm Warbler

The back-body action is a real tell-tail sign. If you see a yellowish warbler that wags its tail up and down constantly, you're likely looking at a Palm Warbler. Like any other warbler, it fits in the palm of your hand.

Orange-crowned Warbler

This is not a bird to write home about.

"Yeah, yeah, no, I saw it too, the yellow. Yeah it had yellow on it."
—Owen

Yellow-throated Warbler
Yellow Warbler
m.
American Redstart
m.
f.
m.
Palm Warbler
tail wag
Black-and-white Warbler
f.
Orange-crowned Warbler

Merritt Island

On July 16th, 1969, three brave men allegedly strapped themselves to a missile and went on the greatest camping trip of all time. On January 16th, 2024, two brothers who had just camped at a Cracker Barrel went birdwatching. Merritt Island is home to Kennedy Space Center and a big wildlife refuge. It's a great place to see birds *and* space stuff.

Tree Swallow  

Ain't a whole lotta swallowing with these guys, from what I've seen at least.

Purple Martin   

A lot of them live in subsidized housing, actually.

Florida Scrub Jay  

I've got something in common with this bird. We both hate golf courses. I hated golf before I got into birds. It's a stupid game for grown-up babies, and it takes up way too much space. Looking for a new place to sink a putt? Try your own a*ss! The Florida Scrub Jay was the first scrub jay we encountered for the year, and the only one considered endangered. While we were on our way to find it, a man endangered our lives by passing us on a two-lane road going about 130 mph. Must've been late for his tee time.

American Flamingo  

We didn't know you could see a flamingo anywhere in the United States outside of a zoo. We went to a spot on the island where you could see them from a few hundred yards away, straight into the sun. Terrible looks. While we were there, we met a woman who had a hard-on for some guy called Kenn Kaufman. This was the first we'd heard of him, but we now know he's a legend and a pioneer in the birding community. She told us all about him, as well as a festival in Ohio that he's part of—The Biggest Week in American Birding. Because of that interaction, we'd end up attending the festival in the spring, where she introduced us to the legendary birdwatcher himself.

m.
Tree
Swallow
cloacal
kiss
f.
apartment
Purple
Martin
Florida
Scrub
Jay
not to scale
American
Flamingo

Marsh Mix

Common Gallinule

Absolutely massive shoes to fill.

Purple Gallinule

Similar to the Common Gallinule, but different enough that you should be able to tell them apart. If you can't, then maybe this whole birding thing isn't for you—and that's okay. There are plenty of other hobbies out there to keep your mind off the impending heat death of the universe.

Grey-headed Swamphen

Another chicken-like marsh bird for ya. These are non-native, but that's okay. No one's throwing around the "I" word just yet.

Snail Kite

The introduction and rapid spread of the non-native Apple Snail has inadvertently helped the well-being of these birds, as well as the Limpkin. They should just make more Snail Kites to take care of the snail problem—easy fix. Snail Kites fu*cking love snails. We saw about six of them hunting for foreign gastropods at a sewage pond one evening. See: Limpkin.

Sedge Wren

Neither of us had heard of *sedge* before we started birdwatching—one of many new words we picked up. *Sedge* sounds like *sludge* and *edge* put together, which is actually where we found one of these birds—by the edge of some sludge.

Common Yellowthroat

Angry little bandits.

Wilson's Snipe

Usually a *snipe* is when you go bar down from 40ft out. In this case, it's actually a shorebird that probes mud with its long beak in search of small invertebrates.

Purple Gallinule
Common Gallinule
Grey-headed Swamphen
Snail Kite
Wilson's Snipe
Sedge Wren
Common Yellowthroat
m.

Longleaf Pines

On these first couple trips, we didn't bring any weed with us. Florida and Texas weren't stoked on the stuff at the time, and we figured we could just get high on birds. A couple weeks in, I was looking for some way to change my consciousness. At every gas station they sell nicotine pouches—little pillows full of nicotine salt that you tuck in your lip. I bought a can and we went birding. First your gum stings, then your vision sharpens, and you're fired up, you could do anything—you're buzzing. Then you have to take a shi*t, and it's an emergency. You're quickly digging a shallow hole in the sand while a hundred business ideas fly through your head. Next thing you know it's nap time, but your heart rate's still at 120 and you have no clue where your brother went. I wouldn't say I'm an advocate.

Pine Warbler   

Kind of a forgettable warbler, if I'm being honest. It wasn't the highlight of the year, but it's fine. It's a small, unimpressive creature. People just don't get excited about birds like this. They probably don't make many stuffed animals of Pine Warblers, but that doesn't mean they're any less important than other, flashier birds.

Red-cockaded Woodpecker   

Overdosed on nicotine, talked to a man on a horse, and made tacos all while waiting around for these endangered woodpeckers.

Brown-headed Nuthatch   

Squeaky little dudes that hatch nut aggresively.

Chipping Sparrow   

Another lipper for the chipper.

Yellow-bellied Sapsucker   

Sounds like a slur, but it's actually the name of a woodpecker-like bird.

"I'll be birding horizontally for a while."
—Owen

Red-cockaded
Woodpecker
Pine
Warbler
f.
Brown-headed
Nuthatch
Yellow-bellied
Sapsucker
f.
Chipping
Sparrow

Loose Change

As we wrapped up our first trip to Florida, we picked up the loose change, payed our tolls with it, and buzzed on out.

Chuck-will's-widow   

We got word that one of these night birds was hanging out at a little nature center. The folks who worked there called it "Wally." The center was going to close for a wedding in less than 30 minutes, so we had to be quick. We weaseled around the suits and dresses, apologizing for our stench, and made our way to a boardwalk in the forest where Wally was said to be roosting. These birds blend into their surroundings and stay very still during the day, making it quite the challenge. With only minutes to spare, Owen spotted Wally. Owen was not the leading bird finder, but when the pressure was on, under the bright lights—that's when he performed his best. This is his depiction of the bird.

Cedar Waxwing  

The squad runs deep—rarely are they alone. Listen for a bunch of high-pitched *tseees* and *weeees*, and you just might find yourself a flock.

House Wren   

Loud, bubbly, musical, chaotic song.

Blue-grey Gnatcatcher  

Weezy little dudes.

Winter Wren  

Short, stubby and dark.

Ovenbird   

350 degrees for 25 minutes, or until golden brown.

"Birdwatching is an old person's game. What do old people do? They sit down, take meds, eat pudding, and birdwatch."
—Owen Reiser

Cedar Waxwing
Chuck-will's-widow
artist's depiction
Blue-grey Gnatcatcher
m.
House Wren
Ovenbird
Winter Wren

First Texas

Late January - Mid February

Duration: 18 days
Distance: 3,151mi
New Birds: 62
Total Birds: 250
Cracker Barrel Stays: 10

General Route: West along the gulf and down the coast to the Rio Grande Valley. Back north to Monroe, LA. Then home to St. Louis.

Significant Places: Galveston Island, Bolivar Flats Shorebird Sanctuary, Aransas NWR, Laguna Atascosa NWR, Dick Kleberg Park, UTRGV, Brownsville, Harlingen, Resaca de la Palma State Park, Bentsen-Rio Grande Valley State Park, Salineño Wildlife Preserve, Corpus Christi, Tensas River NWR

Weather: Hot, sunny, windy

Overview

We'd survived Florida, and we were ready to mess with Texas. It took us a couple days to drive across the coast, but we made it with no issues. There wasn't much of a reason to stop until we hit the Lone Star State. Naturally, our first stop was a Cracker Barrel in Beaumont—probably the dinkiest one we'd stay at all year. Another night at a CB in Corpus Christi, we watched them evacuate the restaurant and cart someone off on a stretcher. I guess the country gravy finally got 'em. Texas has even less public land than Florida. There were a couple of great free outdoor spots, like Bolivar Flats and a random park or two, but it was mostly boondockin' at the Barrel—and that starts to weigh on you.

We knew we had to get down to the Rio Grande Valley, which is where all the good specialty birds are at. The closer to the border you get, the better the birding gets. We didn't know it until we arrived, but it was a great year for the RGV—lots of rare birds were showing up. This meant there were a lot of birders in town from all over the country. We'd met a couple birders in Florida, but the RGV is where we first got a real glimpse into the culture. Seemed like everywhere we went there was someone with a big camera lens or a spotting scope, just itching to tell someone what they saw, or what they know about specific birds. This was to our advantage.

Bolivar Flats

In Texas, you can drive on the beach—so we did. We took the minivan up and down the Bolivar Peninsula, careful not to run over any birds. You can camp there for free too. The cool ocean breeze, the rolling waves, and the twinkling lights of offshore oil rigs will carry you gently to sleep.

Iceland Gull

An uncommon first-winter seagull we identified with care. As if seagulls weren't tough enough already, you should know it takes a few years for them to reach full adult plumage—muddying the waters of identification. At this point, you could say we were in pretty deep. Just north of where we saw that white bird parked in the sand, we noticed a white SUV parked in the sand. Two weeks later, we saw the same vehicle again, in the same spot, when we stopped to camp on our way back north from the Rio Grande Valley at the end of this trip. We'd see it a third time ten months later.
See: Lesser Black-backed Gull.

Stilt Sandpiper

It's a really tall Dunlin. See: Dunlin.

Snowy Plover

Small plover, no snow in sight
Steadily ploving from left to right

Piping Plover

Cutest fu*ckin' little plover out there—almost pi*sses me off.

Neotropic Cormorant

This small cormorant marked the beginning of a series of tough events for myself. The night after we saw one for the first time, I sliced my finger open to the bone with a dull knife while cooking dinner in the van. I was wounded, but I would still be able to complete the computer tasks I was assigned for the day. Up to this point, I was still working remotely for the Bitcoin mining outfit. Somewhere, while fumble-fu*cking around on the keyboard with my freshly filleted phalange, I made a simple mistake. I typed a 1 instead of a 0.

Iceland Gull
first winter
Stilt
Sandpiper
nb.
Snowy
Plover
nb.
Neotropic
Cormorant
Piping
Plover
nb.

It's All Over Fast

Long-billed Curlew

Curl-bill long bird. Curl bird, long curl, bill long, curled-billed longbill.

Whimbrel

Similar to a curlew, but the bill leaves something to be desired.

Marbled Godwit

A Marbled Godwit is a decently sized shorebird with a noticeably upturned bill. God is a guy we went to go see at a church in Houston. One day, Owen alerted me that we could go see Joel Osteen, the bajillionaire motel televangelist, live and in person at Lakewood Church. On a Sunday morning at 10 a.m., we stood in the crowd of the Houston Rockets' old stadium to hear the word of God. Someone in the lobby told me that you could actually meet Joel Osteen after the service. What an opportunity this would be. We left the service a few minutes early so I could be first in line to meet this liaison of God's. I shook his dainty little hand with my unwounded hand, and he told me he would be praying for me. What an advantage this would be—to have God on our side now. Filled with the Holy Spirit, we herded ourselves back to the parking garage, where I received a phone call. The phone call was from a very angry bajillionaire—and not the man I'd just been blessed by. This was the owner of the Bitcoin mining facility. He informed me that the commands I sent to the mining rigs the night before had resulted in a fire and the destruction of a couple hundred thousand dollars' worth of equipment. I was also informed that I was now unemployed. From the highest of highs to the lowest of lows, this is a day I'll never forget.

American Avocet

A pompous bird that thinks it's better than everyone. I'm surprised it's ever hungry, since it's so full of itself.

Black-necked Stilt

A suspicious amount of leg. You should see them try to sit down.

Long-billed
Curlew
Whimbrel
Marbled
Godwit
nb.
Black-necked
Stilt
American
Avocet
legs
nb.

Marshing Onward

Gull-billed Tern

The scientists at the R&D lab retrofitted a seagull bill onto a tern—and it was a huge hit.

Ringed Kingfisher

We watched a pair of these birds fly from Mexico into the United States—Border Patrol nearby, seemingly unworried. But when I do it, it's a huge deal. Birds, obviously, aren't bound by the same system of rules we higher primates are.

White-faced Ibis

Pretty similar to the Glossy Ibis we saw in Florida. The White-faced Ibis does not sport the white face in its nonbreeding plumage. See: Glossy Ibis.

Whooping Crane

The Whooping Crane is a really big bird. They're endangered, so they all wear Fitbits to stay on top of their health. We asked a big, sloppy guy at a wildlife drive where the "hooting" cranes were at, and he said, "No, no, no, wrong spot. Listen, you're gonna wanna go down here, take this side road, bridge, turn here, pass the pavilion, turn here, 4 p.m., big field, line of cars." So we listened to the guy—and he was right on the money.

Sora

 A sight for Sora eyes. A small, chicken-like marsh bird in the rail family. Pretty brave for a rail, in our experience—we've seen them out in the open multiple times. If you're unable to locate one visually, that's okay—they're also audibly pleasing. We once held up traffic at a marsh just to get a good look at one.

Least Grebe

Least, but certainly not last. We would find more grebes throughout the year, but none smaller than this.

Gull-billed
Tern
nb.
Ringed
Kingfisher
f.
White-faced
Ibis
nb.
Whooping
Crane
Sora
Least
Grebe
health computers

City Slickers

Ruby-throated Hummingbird

If you see a hummingbird east of the Mississippi, it's probably this one.

Wilson's Warbler

Small yellow bird adorned with a black cap. Possibly religious.

Chihuahuan Raven

 On the bird software, this raven had been reported at the Brownsville Dump, and the software said it was rare, so we figured we should go check it out for ourselves. We got to the dump and checked in with a very enthusiastic man who gave us some high-vis and a few safety tips. We had a blast tossing our trash out of the van on the way up the mound. The peak proved to be loud, windy, dusty, and stinky. The place was an absolute dump. Breathing conditions were not ideal, but after about 30 minutes we picked a single raven out of the thousands of other garbage-eating birds and got the he*ck out. We would later see these ravens again in a much cleaner and more natural setting in New Mexico. It was worth it for the experience, I guess.

Green Parakeet

More loose pets.

Red-crowned Amazon

One evening, about 200 of these parrots came in to roost at a Brownsville soccer park. There were nearly the same number of kids running around while adults yelled at them in Spanish. We made tacos and watched the show.

Great-tailed Grackle

 We went out of our way to find these birds. We saw on the bird software that they were reported at a nearby park, so we made a 40-minute trip just to see them—not knowing we'd end up encountering them at every gas station west of the Mississip'. A great indication of our knowledge and planning.

m.
Ruby-throated
Hummingbird
f.
Wilson's
Warbler
pizza
Chihuahuan
Raven
m.
Green
Parakeet
Red-crowned
Amazon
f.
Great-tailed
Grackle
m.
Loads

The Phoebe Jeebies

Couch's Kingbird

The same big sloppy guy who gave us directions to the Whooping Cranes told us this bird is called a "Cooses" Kingbird. But you don't go home and sit on the fu*ckin coose now, do you?

Tropical Kingbird

You can see a bird with the word *Tropical* in its name in a Cracker Barrel parking lot, of all places.

Dusky-capped Flycatcher

Owen caused a pompous young birder and her parents to miss this bird, apparently rare for the time and place. Owen and I were with a small group of old people, as was often the case. We were standing quietly, observing the bird, when the girl and her parents showed up, all business—rushed, anxious, aggressive, clearly just there to tick any boxes they could. She pressed Owen about what we were looking at. Not knowing it was a rare bird for the area—and not really caring to serve them in any way, since they didn't come in with great energy—Owen said, *"Ehhh, some flycatcher, I think."* Then they moved on, assuming it was just a common bird. Oops.

Black Phoebe

We first saw one sitting on the branches of the log stuck out in the middle of the Rio Grande. Was it in the United States or Mexico? *Ripping a joint* "They're all just arbitrary human boundaries, maaaaaaan."

Say's Phoebe

Flycatchers will perch up, then fly off as soon as you get your camera or binoculars honed in. You'll be disappointed—but wait. Flycatchers will often return to the very same perch. This is called *sallying*. It *sallied* out for an insect. At the spot where we first saw this bird, we met a man who taught us another "s" word: *skulky*. It means a bird is kinda shy and likes to stay hidden in dense vegitation. We didn't notice him until he himself crawled out of some bushes. God, that guy was a weirdo.

Tropical
Kingbird
Couch's
Kingbird
Dusky-capped
Flycatcher
Say's
Phoebe
Black
Phoebe

It's Hot And Dry

Ladder-backed Woodpecker

The Ladder-backed Woodpecker is like a southwestern version of a Downy Woodpecker—small and patterned with black and white. The male has a red cap. The female does not. If you say *"Ladder Back"* with the right inflection, it can sound like a slur, so be mindful of that. See: Downy Woodpecker.

Golden-fronted Woodpecker

I just don't like em, ya know. They look like they're cheaply made or something. Not the highest quality woodpecker, I don't think. See: Red-bellied & Gila Woodpecker.

Bewick's Wren

My least favorite wren by far. It's not a bad bird by any means, I just like all the other wrens more.

Long-billed Thrasher

It's actually not the thrasher with the longest bill.

Curve-billed Thrasher

There are other thrashers with bills that are arguably more curved.

Western Meadowlark

Pretty much the same as the Eastern Meadowlark, but with a different song. Their song doesn't jazz me up quite the same way, but it's not bad. There are places in Texas where Eastern, Western, and Chihuahuan Meadowlarks can overlap. Take special care to count the outer tail feathers to distinguish them from the Chihuahuan Meadowlark. Western and Eastern both have three white outer tail feathers on each side, whereas the Chihuahuan has four. See: Eastern, Chihuahuan Meadowlark.

Pyrrhuloxia

Essentially a desert cardinal with a fancy name.
See: Northern Cardinal.

Ladder-backed Woodpecker
f.
Golden-fronted Woodpecker
f.
m.
Bewick's Wren
Long-billed Thrasher
Curve-billed Thrasher
1
2
3
tail
Western Meadowlark
Pyrrhuloxia
m.

Boom Chachalaca

Altamira Oriole

There's nothing that drains me quite like sitting at a bird feeder with a bunch of old people. It absolutely kills me.

Green Jay

Egregiously patterned jay. They really pigged out on this one.

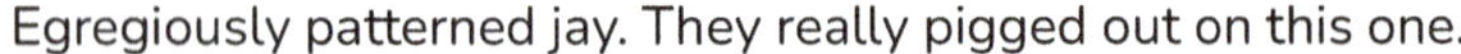

Great Kiskadee

Exotic looking flycatcher—head boldly patterned with black and white. I got tired of the noises they make pretty quickly.

Black-crested Titmouse

The most striking titmouse we could turn up. Nearby, a bald man was doing some sort of cop dog training with one of those dogs you need a license for. He was checkin' us out pretty hard, like he was just dying to let his beast loose any chance he could get. The good news was we didn't have any drugs on us at the time, so there was nothing to worry about. Still, I never feel at ease around a dog like that—or a squatty, bald man.

Plain Chachalaca

It's like a long, malnourished chicken or something. I struggled to photograph one of these birds. It seemed like every time I got an opportunity, someone with a kid would walk right in the way, so I'd have to make sure I wasn't pointing my camera anywhere near them. This was early on, and I was still dead set on getting a picture of every bird—but I lacked composure. One afternoon at Bentsen–Rio Grande Valley State Park, we were having a tough, hot day, and I missed another photo opportunity. No worries. We thought we could rent bikes at the park, but they said it was too late. All good. At least they had showers at one of the campgrounds. The water was brown, and there were four cockroaches at my feet. Tough to say it was worth the five bucks.

Common Pauraque

A nightbird of South Texas. During the day, they just chill on the ground in invisible mode—expertly camouflaged.

Altamira Oriole
Green Jay
Black-crested Titmouse
Great Kiskadee
Plain Chachalaca
Common Pauraque

Resaca de la Naughty

 Resaca de la Palma is a great state park near Brownsville. We found out about it through the Ivy League bird software—there'd been a very rare bird reported there called a *Becard.* When we showed up, we didn't exactly behave ourselves. For starters, we didn't pay the $8 entrance fee. We thought it was one of those things that was more of a suggestion. We were standing in a bird blind—a wooden structure meant to hide you from birds. Thinking we were alone, I started saying some *really* naughty stuff to make Owen laugh. Two minutes later, just to my left behind the thin wooden wall, I heard a shoe scuffle and, through the crack, saw a man walking away. He had been there the entire time. We had to leave immediately. The next day, we decided to press our luck and return. This time we met a small group also looking for the rare bird, so we teamed up. After 20 minutes or so of searching, a white truck approached. It was a park-owned vehicle. It stopped, and a park employee built like a cigarette machine got out. He started birding with us using his tiny binoculars. The binoculars were regular-sized—he was just a brick shi*t house. He immediately pointed out a Tropical Parula, then said, *"Oh, and the Becard just showed back up right behind it."* This guy was incredible. For his final act, he turned to Owen and me and sternly said, *"You guys have a blue minivan, right? You didn't pay the entrance fee. Go pay it before you leave."*
Yes sir.

Tropical Parula   
A brightly-colored little warbler, considered rare in the U.S.

Grey-collared Becard  
Extremely rare in the U.S.—occurring only a handful of times.

Verdin   
Hard little workers. They put in big minutes—always grinding.

Blue-headed Vireo  
Built-in protective headwear. See: Black-capped Vireo.

Western Tanager   
Pointed out to us by a man with a mustache full of snot.

Tropical Parula
m.
Grey-collared Becard
m.
Verdin
Blue-headed Vireo
m.
Western Tanager
m.

Hawks & Doves

Harris's Hawk

 We met a sloppy man with an exposed buttcrack who took wild baby hawks from nests and made them do what he wanted—or tried to, at least. It seemed as if his hawk, a Harris's Hawk named *Tony Hawk*, didn't respect him. We went out hunting rabbits in residential areas with him and Tony to see what it was all about. Most of the time was spent trying to retrieve the bird from people's rooftops using a dead rabbit on a string. The whole thing didn't sit well with us and I can't look at one of these hawks without thinking about the experience.

Grey Hawk

It is grey.

White-tailed Hawk

Pulled over on the side of a highway. Birding while driving was starting to become a safety concern.

Aplomado Falcon

These are some pixels I graphed while we watched a pair of these falcons hanging out on a nesting platform from hundreds of yards away. While we were there, we made tacos in a small dirt parking lot next to a loud road. It was very windy. A man who used to work on solid rocket engines came by, and we talked about some of the birds we'd seen. He may have been CIA.

White-winged Dove

Used to think the song went: *Just like a one-winged dove, flies around in tiny circles. Ooo baby oo, said oo.*

Inca Dove

Small and scaly looking.

White-tipped Dove

Just the tip.

Harris's Hawk
Grey Hawk
Aplomado Falcon
White-tailed Hawk
White-winged Dove
White-tipped Dove
Inca Dove

In The Weeds

A lot of sparrows prefer to stay out of sight, but we noticed early on that they respond well to playback. *Playback* refers to playing sound recordings of a bird you'd like to summon. It's considered an ethical grey area in the birding community. Our use—and occasional abuse—would evolve throughout the year.

Cassin's Sparrow   

I forgot we even saw one of these—that probably tells you everything you need to know.

Lincoln's Sparrow   

The Land of Lincoln? More like the Land of *Thinkin'*. Knowledge is power—stay in school.

Lark Sparrow   

Fashionable bird. Sharp and bold facial patterning—crisp and clean. They did a wonderful job with this one.

Vesper Sparrow   

Look for the thin white eye ring. Then look to make sure you're not on someone's private property searching for small brown birds.

Nelson's Sparrow   

To see a bit of creamy orange on a sparrow—boy, what a treat.

Olive Sparrow   

Special sparrow of south Texas. Didn't see it doin' much other than kinda slowly walkin' along the ground, not in much of a hurry at all.

Seaside Sparrow   

At the start of the jetty at Bolivar Flats, there exists one of the worst portable potties on the planet. While I was blasting playback out into the tall grass, Owen was fighting one of his toughest battles of the year in a wretched plastic box by the sea. Later, he came out shell-shocked but eventually got his eyes on this dumpy little sparrow as well.

Cassin's Sparrow
Lincoln's Sparrow
Lark Sparrow
Vesper Sparrow
Nelson's Sparrow
Seaside Sparrow
Olive Sparrow

Barred Core

Cattle Tyrant

This Brazilian bird took up residence at an oyster bar in Corpus Christi, Texas. As we watched it eat crumbs off the ground, we were on speakerphone with a man who said he could take us out looking for an extinct woodpecker in Louisiana, so we'd head there next. As for the Cattle Tyrant, the ABA court ruled that the bird had traveled to the U.S. by ship and could only be counted as a *provisional* bird on everyone's lists. How they knew it hitched a ride, I'm not sure. But unless someone forced it onto the ship, it still traveled to the United States on its own initiative. That's just working smart, not hard. The bird stuck around the same block for months before vanishing. Everyone assumed it died—or hopped another ship to some-where else. Seven months later, it was back. Someone found it again at the same oyster bar. What a legend.

Barred Owl

Song: *Who gon' cook it? Who cooks for you?*

Ivory-billed Woodpecker

The Louisiana man claims he's seen one on at least five occa-sions. He's also a disbarred lawyer. We were to meet him at a Circle K outside of Monroe at 4 a.m. The night before, Owen was stricken with the flu and opted to take a double dose of NyQuil in a Cracker Barrel parking lot. In the morning, we thought we were going to be late, but it turns out a disbarred lawyer isn't that punctual either. Being the outdoorsman he is, we expected him to roll up in a big pickup truck. We were surprised to see a banged-up little hatchback with no hubcaps and an exhaust leak peeling into the parking lot. We spent nearly four hours with him, trudging through the swamp as the sun came up—stopping, listening, looking for signs of recent tree work. This was all a nightmare for Owen, who was still sick and high on Nyquil. We did not end up seeing the bird, but we did appreciate the man's time, knowledge, and passion for conservation.

Wood Duck

Expertly-patterned duck. Screams as it flies through the woods.

Cattle
Tyrant
Barred
Owl
m.
disbarred lawyer
Ivory-billed
Woodpecker
f.
Wood
Duck
m.

Minnesota

Late February

Duration: 8 days
Distance: 1,739mi
New Birds: 20
Total Birds: 270
Cracker Barrel Stays: 1

General Route: North through IL to Madison, WI, then Duluth, and up to the Sax-Zim Bog area. Back down the same way.

Significant Places: Madison, Lake Waubesa, Yahara River, Sax-Zim Bog, Warren Nelson Memorial Bog, Admiral Rd., Highway 7, Byrns Greenhouse, McDavitt Park, Duluth.

Weather: Cold as shi*t. Cloudy and grey, but decently dry.

Overview

 In late February, we buzzed up north for a short trip to Minnesota. We spent almost all of our time at the **Sax-Zim Bog**. It might sound like a non-binary swamp, but it's actually an expanse of forests, bogs, meadows, and more—covering an area larger than Disney World. The organization that protects it is called Friends of Sax-Zim Bog, and the founder and Executive Director is a goofy man named Sparky. Sparky is a birder, an author, a naturalist, and a he*ck of a photographer. He's the man.

The Sax-Zim Bog is free, which is a great model because it doesn't gatekeep people from enjoying nature. You get to see the place without forking over $17 per person right off the bat. If you feel inclined to donate—which you probably will—you can. But if you don't have the means, you can still enjoy what they've done with the place. If you give them $25, you're considered a **Bog Buddy**, and they'll print your name in a magazine just for that. It's worth it. If you give them $5,000, they'll erect a bench with your name on it. Benches don't cost $5,000, but the money helps protect the Sax-Zim Bog and nearly four thousand species of critter.

We'll get one of those benches someday, but not this time. This time we slept at the hockey rink in the minivan on the north side of the bog. McDavitt Park, it's called, and it has a perfectly dinky outdoor rink as well as a warming house—a small brick building with a fireplace inside. Knowing that we'd be in Minnesota in the winter, we packed our skates and sticks, of course. We'd wake up in the morning, have a rip on the ODR, and then go look for birds all day long. In the evening, we'd have another rip on the ODR, then make a fire and a meal in the warming house.

This was a great trip—no major issues, no injuries—and at only eight days in length, there wasn't enough time to get grumpy. The only thing that pi*ssed me off was just how incredibly nice and welcoming Minnesotans are. What is wrong with these people?

Bog Log

Red Crossbill

We actually ran into the world's leading expert on crossbills on this trip. He specifically studied their calls. We told him we'd just encountered some Red Crossbills and played our recording. He heard one chirp and immediately said, *"Oh yeah, that's definitely call type 12A."* Holy smokes, bud.

Bohemian Waxwing

We drove around Duluth for 3 hours to track down a flock.

Evening Grosbeak

Saw them in the morning.

Purple Finch

It's red in real life.

Canada Jay

Gotta be the most forgettable jay. Missed the whole blue memo.

Redpoll

At the time, there were two kinds: Common Redpoll and Hoary Redpoll. We made sure to give it a proper effort and pick out both kinds—a bird in the flock was worth two on the scoreboard. A few months later, the bird scientists decided there was only one kind. Dash one for the boys. You get tough bounces in this game sometimes, and you just have to put them behind you and keep moving forward. Way she goes.

Black-capped Chickadee

Chickadees are just some of the boys.

Red-breasted Nuthatch

I know, you're seeing the word *breast* there. Don't even think about it. This is a serious book for the purpose of learning.

Pine Siskin

Possibly the dumpiest bird they make. I get mad when I see one.

Red
Crossbill
m.
right
over
left
Bohemian
Waxwing
Evening
Grosbeak
m.
Purple
Finch
m.
Canada
Jay
Redpoll
m.
hoary
Black-capped
Chickadee
Red-breasted
Nuthatch
m.
Pine
Siskin
offgas

Northern Killers

Rough-legged Hawk

They hover over open areas to find prey. This year was what one guy deemed an *irruption* year, meaning there were many more than usual—not that they were oozing molten rock or anything.

Northern Shrike

Northern cousin of the Loggerhead Shrike.
See: Loggerhead Shrike

Snowy Owl

Our first day at Sax-Zim Bog, while we were driving down to the visitors center from the hockey rink, we saw a group of 30 or more parked cars lining the highway. A ways off to the right was a large white bird at the top of a tree, with a crowd of people below pointing large cylinders straight up at it. Photographers. Some were creeping closer and closer, crossing train tracks to get there. One guy even fell and dropped his camera on the tracks while a train was coming. I mean, the train wasn't that close—but it *was* coming. Not but two weeks later, it was reported that the young male owl had apparently been killed by a train. May he rest in peace, or go on to prosper in other dimensions.

Great Grey Owl

 One evening, we followed a bird guide van because we knew exactly what they were after, and that they'd probably succeed. Why pay for the tour when you can just follow it around for free? We tailed the van for about an hour, and just as it was getting too dark to see birds, it stopped. A dozen folks poured out. We knew they had it. We joined the group in observing the silhouette of a large owl and realized there was an aura to this bird. It was such a special sighting that two elderly men embraced in the middle of the road. Others shook hands and thanked the guide—a man named Alex, who's an absolute freak for birds. We'd see him again a couple more times during the year.

Northern Hawk-Owl

Grumpy Gus over here.

Rough-legged Hawk
im.
Northern Shrike
Snowy Owl
m.
R I P
Great Grey Owl
Northern Hawk-Owl
nature guide
WIDESLIDE NATURE TOURS
beep beEep beep

Spark Plug

Black-backed Woodpecker

We met Sparky at the Warren Nelson Memorial Bog, which has birds, mammals, a boardwalk, and even a porta-potty. We followed him out into the woods where he had the hookup on an uncommon woodpecker. It was a single female flaking the bark off a tree. The Black-backed Woodpecker has only three toes, just like the American Three-toed Woodpecker. This was the first we'd heard of the latter, and it would be the beginning of a long and tumultuous journey to find it.
See: American Three-toed Woodpecker.

Ruffed Grouse

In the evening, they climb up into trees to eat buds. This is apparently the best time to eat and avoid predation simultaneously.

Common Raven

We didn't find this one at a dump, but I'm sure they love the dump just as much. See: Chihuahuan Raven.

Long-tailed Duck

The one we saw didn't have a long tail. It was a nonbreeding female, pointed out to us by a group of college students on a field trip. Thanks, guys—you've got an A in my book.

Black-billed Magpie

Magpies would be farmers if they were humans.

American Woodcock

 As soon as we got back to the St. Louis area in early March, it was time to find an American Woodcock. Every year around that time, the males begin their displays, which is the easiest way to locate them. At dusk, the male stands in an open area and repeatedly calls—a loud, abrupt *bzeep* or *peent*. After several of those, he explodes skyward, wings whistling as he spirals higher and higher. He then floats back down to roughly the same spot he took off from and repeats the process. Apparently, the females go crazy for this performance.

Black-backed
Woodpecker
f.
Ruffed
Grouse
Common
Raven
f.
nb.
Long-tailed
Duck
Black-billed
Magpie
m.
American
Woodcock

Southwest

Early March - Mid April

Duration: 42 days
Distance: 5,204mi
New Birds: 91
Total Birds: 361
Cracker Barrel Stays: 2

General Route: I-40 west to Albuquerque, south to Las Cruces, west to southeastern Arizona, then to Oceanside, California. Northeast to Flagstaff, back down to southeastern Arizona, then returning via I-40 east.

Significant Places: Glenrio Smoke Shop, San Jon, Bosque del Apache NWR, Organ Mountains, Las Cruces, Chiricahua Mountains, Cave Creek Canyon, Santa Rita Mountains, Patagonia, Harshaw Rd., Harshaw Creek Rd., Nogales, Tubac, Ron Morriss Park, Sweetwater Wetlands, W. Silverbell Rd., Tucson, Phoenix, Prescott, Flagstaff, Yuma, Oceanside, Lake Meredith NRA.

Weather: Ideal.

Overview

Ahhh, the freedom of the West—no longer shackled by Cracker Barrels. We'd only have to use the Barrel twice on this trip, because free camping is everywhere out here. It's still far from luxury—sleeping in a minivan with your brother every night—but it's better than sleeping in a minivan with your brother every night in a parking lot next to the interstate.

This trip was maybe our most fun. We were getting the hang of finding birds, and we were enjoying the quest. We still had plenty of easy-to-find birds on the table, so it wasn't hard yet. We could count on picking up a couple new ones every day, and the change of scenery was nice.

There was also a change in our diet. For the first couple of trips, we ate one pound of ground beef almost every night. We'd make tacos with corn tortillas, 80/20, avocado, and hot sauce. Delicious and cheap—but it would prove to bite back gastrointestinally. Plus, it's a pretty tough look to try to be naturalists while scarfing down a pound of store-bought ground beef every night. The new menu consisted of rice, beans, greens, avocados, and canned tuna. We supplemented with nuts, fruit, and chips. It ended up being cheaper, easier, and healthier.

New Mexico was a pleasant surprise to us. Before birdwatching, we'd only been to Albuquerque—which is a spicy shi*thole. Turns out, there are other parts of the state.

Most of our time was spent in southeastern Arizona, which is a mecca for birdwatching—and geriatric care. I'm not convinced you can call yourself a birdwatcher unless you've spent time in the sky islands.

To New Mexico

Bronzed Cowbird

Head is remarkably square—could be proof of intelligent design.

Brewer's Blackbird

We got our *lifer* in a Starbucks parking lot. *Lifer* means it's the first time you've seen the species in your life.

Lark Bunting

At the first westbound rest stop in Texas off I-40, there are no restrooms—but you can still pee if you need to. About 50 yards to the north, there's a small cattle farm with a dinky old windmill and, at the time, a flock of these birds. We spent 20–30 minutes in The Lab (the minivan) determining what kind of birds they were.

Chihuahuan Meadowlark

At first, we didn't know to be looking for these birds because they weren't in the guidebook we owned—I guess we had the kids' version or something. We did end up finding a big group of meadowlarks. After a bit of research, we learned that distinguishing the Chihuahuan Meadowlark from the Western Meadowlark can be done by voice or by counting the number of white outer tail feathers. Since the birds were silent, we ended up counting feathers on a blurry image in The Lab.
See: Eastern & Western Meadowlark.

American Pipit

More like *American Skip-It*. Not impressed.

Mexican Duck

Song: *¡Pinche gobernment!*

Eared Grebe

Careful what you say around it—with ears like that.

Cinnamon Teal

Cinnamon Teal, Cinnamon Teal, Cinnamon Teal.

Brewer's
Blackbird
Bronzed
Cowbird
Lark
Bunting
m.
f.
Chihuahuan
Meadowlark
meadowlark
tail
1 2 3 4
American
Pipit
Mexican
Duck
m.
Eared
Grebe
br.
Cinnamon
Teal
m.

Who Knew, New Mexico

Woodhouse's Scrub Jay

Scrub jay two of four.

Ruddy Ground Dove

More like a Ruddy *Found* Dove. Thanks to the very specific directions and detailed instructions from an Ivy League bird software user, we found two of these birds roosting in a tree on the side of a busy road in Las Cruces. We could've sent this bird mail if we wanted to.

Bushtit

Are you serious...

Lesser Goldfinch

Small bird. Male is dark above, yellow below. No qualms.

Gambel's Quail

We spent most of a morning looking for these quails around Bosque del Apache, thinking they'd be extremely shy and hiding in the tall grass. No luck. But when we went to the visitors center to use the bathroom, we saw a dozen of them just hanging around the building, unfazed by humans. We still had no clue which birds were going to be easy to see, and which ones we'd have to really put time and effort into searching for. A grizzled veteran of a birder would know not to worry about looking for these quails—you're going to run into them often in the Southwest.

Rock Wren

Wrock on brother.

"I thought it was all just meth and nukes before this whole bird thing."
—Owen

Woodhouse's Scrub Jay
Ruddy Ground Dove
Bushtit
Lesser Goldfinch
m.
Rock Wren
m.
Gambel's Quail

Cave Crick Canyon

When we stepped out of the van for the first time in Cave Creek Canyon, we heard a distant *"Help!"* It was an old man in a powered wheelchair, stuck in the mud. We pushed him out, and he offered us birding tips in return—as long as we didn't tell his wife he got stuck. His secret was safe with us. Bill was a wealth of knowledge, and quite the character.

Bridled Titmouse

Travel in tight little posses, ringing about.

Black-throated Blue Warbler

"God, what a beautiful bird. An absolute beacon." —Bill

Painted Redstart

Possibly the best warbler they've ever made.

Elegant Trogon

Bill told us exactly where and when to see this bird. He said it would show up to eat a couple berries at Cave Creek Ranch at 4 p.m. He was with us while we waited for it—and so was his wife. Every so often, she'd whisper something in his ear, and he'd grumpily say something back like, *"The same woodpecker I told you it was the last time you asked me!"*

Mexican Jay

Little bit rowdy, these guys. The squad stays tight. They've got each other's backs. Seems like they've got a good thing goin'.

Yellow-eyed Junco

Arguably cooler than the Dark-eyed Junco. See: Dark-eyed Junco.

Montezuma Quail

 Montezuma may not have made a great leader, but he made a great quail. This stunning ground bird looks like royalty with its little hairdo and formal patterning. Owen spotted a pair while we were driving down the canyon one morning. It was one of the birds I wanted to see most, and we got fantastic looks.

Bridled
Titmouse
Black-throated
Blue Warbler
m.
Painted
Redstart
Elegant
Trogon
m.
Mexican
Jay
Montezuma
Quail
m.
Yellow-eyed
Junco

Flicker, Sucker, Pecker

Gila Woodpecker

We went out to a bar in Tucson with some folks one night and had too many beers. We were allowed to crash at their place. I was offered a couch in the living room, so I opted for a break from the van and slept inside. In the middle of the night, I had to pee, so naturally I went out the front door and watered the yard. When I returned, I realized I had locked myself out. Luckily, there was an outdoor couch on the porch, so—rather than wake anyone up—I just went back to sleep there. A few hours later, I was awoken by one of these woodpeckers repeatedly and relentlessly drilling on the metal pipes on the roof, as well as the neighbor's mailbox. This was all a little too much for me at the time.
See: Red-bellied & Golden-fronted Woodpecker.

Red-naped Sapsucker

 Why are sapsuckers a little sneakier than woodpeckers? Is it because they don't want word getting out that they spend their entire waking life tonguin' on sap? Get a grip, guys.

Arizona Woodpecker

It's a brown woodpecker. Not that big, but not that small either. You'd have issues trying to fit it in a Chinese take-out container—for a random hypothetical example. It's called the Arizona Woodpecker, but most of them are in Mexico. It seems like Mexico's kinda gettin' hosed on this one.

Gilded Flicker

The desert cousin of the Northern Flicker. I got a cousin out there too. He tried to kill me with a golf cart when we were kids, but that's all behind us now.

Acorn Woodpecker

Very cool the first time you see one—diminishing returns after that.

Red-naped
Sapsucker
m.
m.
Gila
Woodpecker
Arizona
Woodpecker
f.
Gilded
Flicker
m.
f.
Acorn
Woodpecker

Desert Scrub

Mesquite, Palo Verde, Graythorn, Saguaro—these are all names of plants that have made me bleed. The desert lowlands around the sky islands are full of great birds and spicy plants. West Silverbell Road, northwest of Tucson, is where we found most of these birds—and where we'd get to know them. There's great camping out there. We ended up spending about three weeks total there, scattered throughout the year.

Ash-throated Flycatcher

Pretty large, yellow-bellied bird. Very similar to other flycatchers, but they can all be distinguished by their accents. See: Great Crested, Brown-crested, & Dusky-capped Flycatcher.

Phainopepla

Black desert cardinal type beat. The male is all black with a red eye—the female is more of a dusty grey. A local told us that they will vomit up their stomach lining every so often. No worries.

Cactus Wren

Huge for a wren. How many birds have perished via cactus spine along the evolutionary timeline? Perhaps many—but the modern-day Cactus Wren navigates aggressive plant matter with impunity. Song is deep, harsh, and throaty.

Crissal Thrasher

My Crissal ball tells me I'm gonna be digging another cat hole out here soon.

Black-tailed Gnatcatcher

Gnats? We watched one eat about a hundred ants. Careful with the little red ones.

Greater Roadrunner

 Rockstar. So cool it doesn't bother to fly much. Large, terrestrial bird with a hairdo and a racecar decal behind the eye. Way better in real life than in the cartoon. It's been my favorite bird since the second I laid eyes on one.

Ash-throated
Flycatcher
Phainopepla
m.
Cactus
Wren
Crissal
Thrasher
Black-tailed
Gnatcatcher
m.
br.
Greater
Roadrunner

Hummingbirds

Hummingbirds are tiny little birds that fly around at 100 mph, all cracked out and spazzing on one another as they jockey for position at the sugar water feeder. The Southwest is home to a lot of hummingbirds. Here are a few of them.

Black-chinned Hummingbird

As advertised

Anna's Hummingbird

Anna's, Allen's, Amber's—who gives a shi*t? They're all basically bugs.

Violet-crowned Hummingbird

Seen exclusively at the Paton Center for Hummingbirds in Patagonia, AZ—a place we donated over a dollar to.

Allen's Hummingbird

Extremely similar to the Rufous Hummingbird. You'll need to compare the shape of the tail feathers to tell them apart—or just ask the guy with the giant camera lens. He probably knows. See: Rufous Hummingbird.

Blue-throated Mountaingem

Pretty large for a hummingbird, not that bad.

Rivoli's Hummingbird

Large dark hummingbird. Nearly bird sized. The day we saw this bird for the first time is the day we got our first flat tire of the year. We would get four flat tires in total throughout the year.

Broad-billed Hummingbird

This one's fine I guess. It looks the most delicious out of all the hummingbirds we were able to find.

Costa's Hummingbird

Sounds like a diesel truck. Do *not* fill with diesel—it'll ruin the bird's engine.

Black-chinned Hummingbird
m.
Anna's Hummingbird
m.
Violet-crowned Hummingbird
f./im.
Allen's Hummingbird
m.
Blue-throated Mountaingem
m.
Rivoli's Hummingbird
m.
Broad-billed Hummingbird
f.
Costa's Hummingbird

Swallows et. al.

White-throated Swift

These birds spend their time either flying around catching insects with their face, or hanging out in small cracks in the rocks, high up in the mountains. Sky and crag is all they know. We met a couple climbers around this time that only knew crag. I'd be willing to bet the birds were more intelligent.

Cliff Swallow

Found a crew of these around a canal near Yuma, AZ.

Violet-green Swallow

This bird sparked a controversy in the birding community a few years back—they call it *Swallowgate*. Owen did a bit of investigative journalism for our movie. Birders take the honor system very, *very* seriously.

Northern Rough-winged Swallow

Rest in peace to the Northern Rough-winged Swallow that I killed with the minivan on a highway in Oklahoma. I couldn't do anything about it—I didn't know it was coming. It just flew across the road, right into the grill of the van. We were deeply saddened by this. From then on, I was even more cautious of birds near the road—slowing down when I could, honking the horn to alert them of the vehicle. To our knowledge, this was the only bird death we were directly involved in for the entire year.

Bell's Vireo

A very vocal and relatively tame bird. Allows close approach—but not *too* close.

Hutton's Vireo

Kind of an angry little guy. Confused it with a Ruby-crowned Kinglet on more than one occasion. See: Ruby-crowned Kinglet.

Lucy's Warbler

Drab for a warbler.

White-throated
Swift
Cliff
Swallow
Violet-green
Swallow
Northern
Rough-winged
Swallow
m.
Bell's
Vireo
Hutton's
Vireo
m.
Lucy's
Warbler

Going To California

We drove across the desert to Oceanside, where we stayed for a couple days and then took our friend Joel birdwatching with us on the way back to Arizona. This was a different Joel than the church owner we met in Texas. This was our friend Joel—a man with six pounds of hair and three testicles. We hadn't seen him in over a year and he thought we'd gone insane. This was his first time birdwatching, and he would end up *slightly* enjoying it.

Heermann's Gull

These seagulls are brown when they're young.

Western Gull

Holy smokes, it's *another* seagull.

Western Bluebird

Got our *lifer* at Joel's house. Then we ate weed cereal and got so high we didn't go birding the rest of the day. Compare to the Eastern Bluebird. The rusty orange breast of the Eastern Bluebird doesn't extend over the shoulder like it does on the Western Bluebird. The Eastern Bluebird is also far less likely to be seen at Joel's house. See: Eastern Bluebird.

Western Kingbird

Cassin's Kingbird

Two more nearly identical yellow-bellied kingbirds. Best distinguished by the sounds they make, of course. Kingbirds like open areas with nice perches, where they can launch their aerial assaults on unsuspecting flying insects. See: Tropical & Couch's Kingbird.

Western Grebe

Compare to the similar Clark's Grebe. The Western Grebe has a black cap that extends down and surrounds the red eye. The Clark's Grebe also has a black cap, but it does not extend down to surround the red eye. The eye of the Clark's Grebe is surrounded by white. Also note habitat: you're more likely to find a Clark's Grebe at an all-women's prison.
See: Clark's Grebe.

first winter
Western Gull
Heermann's Gull
Western Bluebird
m.
f./im.
Cassin's Kingbird
Western Kingbird
Western Grebe

California Grown

Joel is arguably one of the poets of our generation. This is a piece he wrote on birdwatching in the Southwest. It took him about nine minutes to complete.

Searching for birds in the desert where the sun is bright and warm
One hand on my nocs, while the other rests upon my great horn
Birds with bright colors, soft hoots, and unique hollers
But if you want to look at them, it will cost you seventeen dollars
Tits, cocks, suckers, and boobies filling the air
Traveling to and from in a Kia Sedona—condition: good to fair
Birds singing in my ears while the Audubon sends an email to whine
Please subscribe to our Patreon for sixteen ninety-nine.
— Joel

Wrentit

"I'd rather own it." - Joel

Mountain Chickadee

Chickadees are just some of the boys.

Nuttall's Woodpecker

California's version of the Ladder-backed Woodpecker. See: Ladder-backed Woodpecker.

Lawrence's Goldfinch

Yes, another type of goldfinch. I've got no qualms with goldfinches of any kind.

Oak Titmouse

It's just a plain grey bird. Don't go out of your way to see it.

California Towhee

California this, California that. Look at all our birds!

California Gnatcatcher

There's no *Missouri* Gnatcatcher, ya know?

California Scrub Jay

They can't be overshadowed by Florida's scrub jay, now can they? *"We'll make our own scrub jay,"* they said!

Wrentit
f.
Nuttall's
Woodpecker
Mountain
Chickadee
Oak
Titmouse
Lawrence's
Goldfinch
m.
California
Scrub Jay
California
Towhee
California
Gnatcatcher
m.

Flagstaff

After birding our way back to Arizona from California, with our friend Joel in tow, we ended up camping in Flagstaff for the night, with plans to go up to the Grand Canyon the next day and hike down to the river. Joel got a booboo on his knee and told us he couldn't go. We decided we'd all stay in town the next day instead and meet up with a stranger at a dog food plant to find some new birds. The stranger ended up being a cute young woman who also hated the French—so we got along great. We all spent the day birdwatching and fu*cking off around town. We found the birds shown here in the Ponderosa pines. Later, the four of us went out to a billiards bar and admired the local body art. Afterwards, our new friend let us sleep on her floor, since a foot of snow was expected overnight. For that, we are grateful.

Lewis's Woodpecker

Dusty old Christmas-themed woodpecker.

Pinyon Jay

They say it's kind of a sensitive species—be careful what you say around them.

Pygmy Nuthatch

Itty bitty little nuthatcher. You could fit 4-6 of them in your mouth with no issues at all.

Townsend's Solitaire

 Kind of like a thrush, kind of like a bluebird. Almost entirely grey. Just on the edge of town is where we laid eyes on one for the first time.

Steller's Jay

A loud jester, like most of the jays we'd come across so far. This one is the most strikingly patterned.

Pinyon
Jay

Lewis's
Woodpecker

Pygmy
Nuthatch

Townsend's
Solitaire

Steller's
Jay

Fruity Lookin' Birds

Streak-backed Oriole

 We made a stop in Phoenix for a day—which is about as long as you want to be there. Phoenix is a huge shopping mall in the middle of an otherwise uninhabitable wasteland. There's a lot of golf and Botox, and when you go outside, it doesn't feel like you're outside—it just feels like they turned the AC off. Surprisingly, there are several parks in the city with a decent number of birds. We were on the search for this oriole, which is considered rare in the United States. While we were there, we met a large man who was roaming the park and drinking vodka at 9 a.m. We talked to him for a while, and he passed on his wisdom to us. Later, we went to our cousin's house and he allowed us to tent camp between the piles of dog shi*t in the gravel side yard. For that, we are grateful.

Hooded Oriole

Hooded means uncircumcised as far as I'm concerned. Possibly a religious bird.

Scott's Oriole

Now batting... number 42... Scott Soriole.

Hepatic Tanager

Better than a hepatitis teenager.

Rosy-faced Lovebird

More loose pets in Phoenix.

Lazuli Bunting

At the Paton Center for Hummingbirds, a man dressed as a cowboy showed up and started chatting with us. We thought maybe he was a poorly trained undercover agent—he didn't look like a cowboy, he was just cosplaying as one. Nonetheless, he pointed out this bird to us. After that, we kept mispronouncing it in different ways just to get under the skin of the other birdwatchers. We are a*ssholes.

Streak-backed
Oriole
Hooded
Oriole
m.
Scott's
Oriole
m.
Rosy-faced
Lovebird
m.
Hepatic
Tanager
m.
Lazuli
Bunting

Southwest Sparrows

Black-throated Sparrow

Very sharply-dressed sparrow.

Rufous-winged Sparrow

Rufous is another advanced way of saying brown. This bird has a small *rufous* patch on the upper wing.

Harris's Sparrow

We saw one next to a pile of sticks.

Rufous-crowned Sparrow

We used playback to get a good look at one of these birds. At this point, we were really starting to hit the playback hard. You can wait and wait and maybe get a good window to view a bird—or you can blast the breeding song from the Ivy League bird software, and that little squirt will pop right up in plain sight for ya. Playback is an addictive drug, and we were starting to abuse it.

Spotted Towhee

Similar to the Eastern Towhee, but this one has white spots on the wings. They also sound different. See: Eastern Towhee.

Brewer's Sparrow

Our encounter with this organism was brief and uneventful.

Abert's Towhee

Large sparrow with a black mask. Call it an "*Albert's*" Towhee to a serious birdwatcher if you'd like to see their blood boil.

Green-tailed Towhee

Saw one next to a pile of sticks.

Canyon Towhee

We saw plenty of these, but one that stood out was a resident of the feeders at Cave Creek Ranch. The bird was missing most of its upper bill but was still grinding out a life, taking advantage of the easy seed—working smart, not hard.

Black-throated
Sparrow
Rufous-winged
Sparrow
Harris's
Sparrow
Rufous-crowned
Sparrow
Spotted
Towhee
Brewer's
Sparrow
f.
Abert's
Towhee
Green-tailed
Towhee
Canyon
Towhee

Southwest Killers

Zone-tailed Hawk 

These are black hawks that soar with Turkey Vultures sometimes—in hopes of blending in. Easily told apart by the trained
eye. Look for a white band on the tail, and then spank your
own a*ss and say, *"Giddy up, I got a new lifer!"*

Common Black Hawk 

We were at Ron Morriss Park for Tubac Hawk Watch (*too-
bok-hok-woch*), when a very serious and tall man, staring
intently through his four-thousand-dollar scope, exclaimed,
*"I've got a Common Black Hawk! If it's a life bird for anyone,
step up to the scope!"* And there it was.

Prairie Falcon 

It's nice to see a falcon, it really is.

Broad-winged Hawk 

Pretty small hawk with short stout wings.

American Goshawk 

These are some pixels I graphed of an individual we briefly
watched ripping down the canyon at Cave Creek Ranch.

Swainson's Hawk 

Look out for a brown band across the chest. Also look out for
snakes. One evening at Sweetwater Wetlands in Tucson, we
spotted a dead ground squirrel next to a pile of sticks. I looked
into the pile and saw a rattlesnake curled up inside—likely
the reason for the squirrel's demise. While we waited to see
if the snake would come out to eat its dinner, an older man
sat down with us and started talking about photography and
living in a car. Before he left, he handed us a slip of paper with
an address on it and told us we could get a shower there for
a buck fifty. It sounded a little dicey, but it turned out to be the
Donna R. Liggens Center—and it's a fine facility. They do a lot
of good for bums.

Zone-tailed
Hawk
Common
Black
Hawk
Broad-winged
Hawk
Prairie
Falcon
American
Goshawk
Swainson's
Hawk

Mining for Birds

Whiskered Screech Owl  

Just outside the town of Patagonia, in the Coronado National Forest right off Harshaw Road, there are a few great camp-sites. It was here that we first found out screech owls don't screech—they toot. The only thing we heard screeching were the brakes of the mining trucks traveling to and from the near-by mines throughout the night.

Elf Owl  

These tiny owls chuckle rather than toot. We never did get eyes on them, but we did get eyes on a mountain lion. One night in the Chiricahuas, we decided to go out after dark with a flashlight and try to track down an owl. We turned a corner on a forest service road and saw the bright yellow eyes of a large mammal looking back at us about 40 yards ahead. We thought maybe it could be a deer, but we noticed the head was round and the ears weren't that big. Something was off. I started clapping and talking a little louder. It didn't run away like a deer—it came closer. We started backing up slowly, kicking gravel, yelling, clapping, and beating our chests. It came to within 25 yards, then darted up a hill to our left with a single stride and without making a sound. I had just smoked a joint before all this, and my heart rate was probably 190. I think we handled it as well as we could have, but moving forward, our night birding would be minimal.

Common Poorwill   

You can see them on the roads at night in the Southwest. A bright-eyed, creepy little lump. Night birds are cool, but they freak me out.

Barn Owl   

There are some old abandoned mine shafts at the foothills of the Santa Rita Mountains. In the day time, if you're careful, you can look down into the shafts and see Barn Owls roosting in there. They don't want you to be there. We took a quick peek, and then got the he*ck out. Again, night birds are cool, but they freak me out.

Whiskered
Screech
Owl
Elf
Owl
Common
Poorwill
cougar
mine
shaft
Barn
Owl

Spring Migration

Mid April - Late May

Duration: 46 days
Distance: 1,866mi
New Birds: 63
Total Birds: 424
Cracker Barrel Stays: 0

General Route: Mainly stayed around the St. Louis area, then headed northeast to Ohio for the Biggest Week in American Birding Festival.

Significant Places: Bohm Woods Nature Preserve, Riverlands Migratory Bird Sanctuary, Greenspace East, MCT Bike Trails, Horseshoe Lake State Park, Lincoln Shields, Centennial Park, Columbia Bottoms CA, Forest Park, Weldon Spring CA, Magee Marsh, Howard Marsh.

Weather: Warm and wet.

Overview

Birds have tiny little magnetic computers in their heads that tell them when and where to go—much like the bajillion-aires would like to install in all of our heads. In the spring-time, many of these birds travel up the Americas to find a suitable place to multiply. Some of them travel from as far as southern Argentina, all the way up to the Arctic. From toe to tip, that's a trip. Depending on where you're at, some of these birds might stick around all summer—or they might just be making a pit stop on their way farther north.

Spring migration is an exciting time, but for me, it turned into a grumpy time. This is where I got sucked into the list-ing game. By this time, we'd racked up a pretty decent list of birds, and it just made me want more. I lost sight of what our real goal was—I just wanted to see the number go up. I wasn't enjoying observing wild animals anymore—I was focused on ticking boxes. When a day went by without a new species, I was a grumpy little dude.

This was me flying too close to the sun. It took one he*ck of a trip on a marijuana edible to get me back down to Earth. From then on out, I didn't worry as much. We were obvious-ly never going to break any records or find any new species, so what was the point in worrying?

We strategically stayed around the St. Louis area for much of the spring, because it's on the Mississippi Flyway, of course. The birds basically just come to you. It seemed like every day there was something new and brightly colored showing up in the local parks. We also went up to Ohio for the annual Biggest Week in American Birding Festival. Our friend Joel joined us again for this leg. We gave ourselves stick-and-poke tattoos for the festival's tattoo contest. We did not win—which was bullshi*t.

Wide Open Spaces

Barn Swallow

This is the best swallow. All the rest of them are cool and all, but this one is the best. They are easily told apart from other swallows by their long forked tails.

Bank Swallow

Known to nest in and around financial institutions. Told from other swallows by the dark band across the neck. This is a sign of the bird's wealth and status.

Chimney Swift

You might go, *"Oh look, a bat,"* but it's not a bat. If you're watching it and watching it and waiting for it to land, you're gonna be there forever—they just don't land. People talk about zero-point energy like it's some far-off mystery, but it's right there above our heads. The Chimney Swift never runs out of energy.

Indigo Bunting

Lay down a good one. Put your teammates in a good position. That's all you're trying to do here.

Northern Bobwhite

This is your go-to quail east of the Mississippi. Listen for a loud two-or three-part whistle. Song: *bob-WHITE or I'm-bob-WHITE.* Can be very hard to spot.

Dickcissel

Named after the late great Richard Cissel, this exquisitely patterned sparrow is a common resident of open country. Song and calls are raspy and buzzy.

"And it's cool with us calling it that?"
—Owen

Barn
Swallow
Bank
Swallow
Chimney
Swift
Indigo
Bunting
m.
showing bunt
Northern
Bobwhite
m.
m.
Dickcissel

Glyphosate Gang

I'd be willing to bet every one of these birds has trace amounts of poison in their brightly colored little bodies. We saw most of them at Forest Park in St. Louis, where we also saw the Glyphosate Gang—aka the Atrazine Army, aka the Poison Platoon—decked head to toe in protective gear and strapped with a few gallons each, spraying anything they'd deemed undesirable. They'll say they're *"managing invasives,"* but the only thing they seem to be managing is a long-term poisoning of our beautiful planet. I think whatever amount of poison you spray out into the environment, you should have to personally ingest an equal amount.

Summer Tanager 

It's not a cardinal, but it is a red perching bird. The male is bright red; the female is more of a dull yellowish-green. You'll hear their calls from the treetops—three descending clicking notes: *dick-a-doo.* That's what it sounds like to me, at least. If you're a novice like me, the song sounds similar to the Rose-breasted Grosbeak and the Baltimore Oriole (below).

Scarlet Tanager 

"If it's anything like Scarlett Johansson, then I'm on board."
—Owen

Blue Grosbeak 

We pronounce it *grōzbeag.*

Rose-breasted Grosbeak 

Seeing a new bird and not knowing what it could be is excit-ing—an adrenaline rush of varying magnitude from person to person. I can tell you that when I saw this bird for the first time, I was rock hard. Rock hard on the inside, in a non-sexual way.

Baltimore Oriole 

World Series Champs: 1966, 1970, 1983

Orchard Oriole 

I would say the female Orchard Oriole is pretty nice, but not *that* nice. They aren't out there making mascots out of them.

Summer Tanager
m.
Scarlet
Tanager
Blue
Grosbeak
f.
m.
m.
Rose-breasted
Grosbeak
Baltimore
Oriole
f.
Orchard
Oriole
m.

Vireos & Flycatchers

Vireos aren't flycatchers, but they do catch flies sometimes. I've seen it with my own eyes.

Warbling Vireo 

Up to this point, we still didn't know what warbling actually meant. Whatever it was, we could assume that this vireo was pretty into it.

Red-eyed Vireo 

The song of the Red-eyed Vireo sounds like the bird is repeatedly asking a question and then quickly answering itself. Could be multiple personality disorder or schizophrenia, but I'm not qualified to make that diagnosis.

Yellow-throated Vireo 

Wears a subtle spectacle. Olive-greenish above, with dark wings and two white wing bars. White below—but the throat is yellow, of course. The song is vaguely similar to other questioning vireos, but a bit raspier, like it's been smoking cigarettes.

Olive-sided Flycatcher 

A decent-sized flycatcher. Apart from the large bill and peaked hairdo, you can distinguish this bird from other flycatchers by the vest it wears. It also has a habit of perching on the highest, most exposed dead branches—*teed up*, as they say.

Eastern Wood Pewee 

Take special care when comparing these flycatchers to the Prima Donna Flycatchers. The song is a two-part question and answer, whistled from forested areas.
Song: *pewee? peee weeeeeee.*

Eastern Kingbird 

Decent-sized flycatcher. Dark above, white below. Note the small white tip on the tail feathers. Voice is loud and high-pitched, with a shrieking quality.

Warbling Vireo
Red-eyed Vireo
Yellow-throated Vireo
Eastern Wood Pewee
Olive-sided Flycatcher
Eastern Kingbird

Wood Warblers

Warblers are tiny birds that hang out in the woods. You could easily fit multiple in your mouth at once. There's an inherent sense of urgency about finding them—they're highly migratory. Depending on your location, they might only be passing through for a couple weeks a year on their way to the breeding grounds. We were told early on that we'd need to search for warblers in the spring. This would be the easiest time to find them. In the spring, the males sing to attract mates, and that's the main way you're alerted to their presence.

Warbling refers to the way the bird sings. Most of it is high-pitched. People describe their various songs as trilly, chortly, buzzy, chattery, zippy, melodic, and so on. As a beginner, this all just tends to blend together. So for us, this meant holding the bird software up to the treetops and seeing what it said was up there. We made sure to double check that our recordings weren't being sent to some Ivy League database—otherwise we'd have some tough hot mic moments to explain.

Hearing them is one thing, but actually *seeing* them is no easy task—warblers are constantly on the move. You're lucky if they stop for more than a second. By this time, all the trees are leafed out, so they pop in and out of view—but mostly out. You gotta find your window without breaking your neck, all while the mosquitoes steal your life juice. Not my favorite style of birding, but it can be rewarding when you do get a good look. Some of these guys have pretty electric paint jobs.

A typical day in the woods might sound like this: *tseep tseep, zit, sEe zee, zee, zee sEe, zee, zip.* What's that one? *tseep chip, cheep, chip.* Uhhhh, hold on. *bzee bzee, veebee vee bee veee, tsip, tsip, seeu, seeu, zee zee, see, zee zee, tsee. chur, chur, chur, zeEeoop.* God*ammit, it's fu*ckin frozen again. *bzee zup, tsie, tsie, twip twip, veeeeeuur, tseep, zeip, bzee bzee. chip, chip.* There, that one up there. Right there. *zip zeep, tseer tseer, zeeeEep, tsip.* No, to the left. *seeu tsee, seeuuuu cheerp cheeerp, bzeet, seep.* Right there. Ow, fu*ck. *veeeebee tseeo tseeo, sip, sip, sip, zee zee, zee zee, tsee sweeeee.* Nevermind, it flew away.

Nashville Warbler

Tennessee Warbler

Kentucky Warbler

Nashville, Tennessee, Kentucky—someone had some serious pull in the birdwatching community down there.

Black-throated Green Warbler

Magnolia Warbler

Northern Parula

Chestnut-sided Warbler

Bay-breasted Warbler

Blackburnian Warbler

A favorite amongst the Amish. We were not surprised to learn that Amish people love birdwatching—we met a few of them in Ohio. They don't use the bird software.

Blackpoll Warbler

Worm-eating Warbler

Cerulean Warbler

Golden-winged Warbler

Blue-winged Warbler

The Blue-winged and Golden-winged Warblers are known to hybridize. Birders and ornithologists get excited when two species interbreed, but when *I* do it, it's a huge deal—there's all these court dates and paperwork, and I'm not allowed to go to the zoo anymore. No one seems nearly as stoked on it.

Mourning Warbler

Prothonotary Warbler

The talk of the boardwalk at Magee Marsh. Most everyone can find one—not everyone can pronounce it.

males
Nashville Warbler
Tennessee Warbler
Black-throated Green Warbler
Kentucky Warbler
Magnolia Warbler
Northern Parula
Chestnut-sided Warbler
Bay-breasted Warbler

Blackburnian Warbler
Blackpoll Warbler
Cerulean Warbler
Worm-eating Warbler
Golden-winged Warbler
Blue-winged Warbler
Prothonotary Warbler
Mourning Warbler

Thrush Rush

Northern Waterthrush  

Louisiana Waterthrush  

These are warblers that walk on the ground and constantly bounce their back halves down and up. The Northern Waterthrush was easy to find, but it took us 10 days to spot a Louisiana Waterthrush, which is brighter white, has pinker legs, and lacks streaking on the throat.
See: The bottom left corner of every page.

Veery  

Veery nice song. Can be veery difficult to see one.

Hermit Thrush  

When compared to the other thrushes on this page, this is the only one with a contrasting reddish tail.

Grey-cheeked Thrush  

Wiry, electric song from an unassuming bird.

Swainson's Thrush  

We saw them first in the Midwest, but we'd see—and hear—them best in the forests of the Pacific Northwest. They kinda run the show up there.

Wood Thrush  

 This bird means a lot to me. It marked a turning point. As I mentioned, spring migration really brought out the demons in me. One night I decided to try a delta-8 THC gummy that was laying around the house. Now, I usually don't fu*ck with any of that synthetic trash, but for some reason I gave it a shot. My entire nervous system vibrated for 36 hours, and all I could think about was how embarrassing it was that I'd been getting grumpy about birdwatching. The next morning, while my bell was still rung, Owen took me to the woods and we found this thrush. The bird's song and the lingering edible made for a psychedelic, Disney-movie-a*ss situation. The song is a few eerily off-tune, melodic notes followed by the sound it makes when you kick one of those springy bathroom doorstops. It's wonderful.

Northern Waterthrush
Louisiana Waterthrush
tail bounce
Veery
Hermit Thrush
Swainson's Thrush
Grey-cheeked Thrush
Wood Thrush

Shore Score And 7 Birds Ago

We observed these birds at Lincoln Shields—a place where Abraham Lincoln nearly killed someone with a sword back in the day. It's a great pit stop for migrating shorebirds.

American Golden Plover

 We saw this bird just to the left of a wiffle ball stuck in the mudflats of the Mississippi River. I'm not sure if wiffle balls are a habitat requirement, but it's a good place to start if you're ever in the market for one of these plovers. See: Black-bellied Plover.

Hudsonian Godwit

Hot and hazy, distant views. Like a Marbled Godwit, but a little more jazzed up. See: Marbled Godwit.

Solitary Sandpiper

Usually seen alone.

Baird's Sandpiper

At a great distance on a hot day, every shorebird out there looks about the same—like a brownish-grey smudge. Look for an elongated smudge with a more horizontal posture than the rest, and you might have yourself a Baird's Sandpiper.

Pectoral Sandpiper

These birds can bench 225 pounds for reps.

Semipalmated Sandpiper

This bird is not *quite* all the way palmated.

White-rumped Sandpiper

 This bird basically travels from the South Pole to the North Pole every year just to get some a*ss. A journey of thousands of miles, and it'll stop for a break not too far from a Dirt Cheap liquor store, where you can see it for yourself. Nearby, we talked to a freelancer who was eating wild berries. *"They won't make you sick or nothin'."* he assured us. We offered to take him birding, but he declined. He'd rather be homeless than do what we were doing.

American
Golden
Plover
nb.
Hudsonian
Godwit
br.
br.
Solitary
Sandpiper
nb.
Baird's Sandpiper
Pectoral
Sandpiper
nb.
Semipalmated
Sandpiper
nb.
br.
White-rumped
Sandpiper
freelancer

Marsh Madness

Franklin's Gull

We saw this one flying over the Missouri River in Alton, near the locks, while we were standing on the Missouri side. After reporting it on the bird software, I got an email saying it was important to change the sighting location to an Illinois hotspot—something about jurisdiction. Yeah, sure buddy, I'll invoice you I guess.

Least Tern

Least, but certainly not last. We would find more species of tern during the year, but none smaller than this.

Black Tern

The black sheep of the tern family. We pulled over on a dirt road near a marsh to have a leak one afternoon, and it just so happened to be way too close to a nesting colony of these guys. We were dive-bombed and screamed at by about a dozen of them. They're good parents.

Least Bittern

 We missed one of these at a park in Phoenix on our previous Southwest trip. It was *"out in the open and being seen well,"* someone told us, but there was also a man at the park drinking vodka at 9 a.m., so we needed to talk to him instead. This time, we heard them far out in the reeds at the local marsh. Occasionally, one would pop up and fly a short distance before diving back into cover—but we wanted a better look. Needing a boat but not having a boat, we each engineered and manufactured our own vessels out of bamboo, painter's tarp, and duct tape. The payoff was almost worth the effort.

Yellow-headed Blackbird

We got our best looks behind a Wal-Mart, but they go to other places too I'm sure.

Franklin's Gull
nb.
br.
Least Tern
Black Tern
br.
Yellow-headed Blackbird
m.
Least Bittern
HMS Bittern
Titan II

Prima Donna Flycatchers

These five birds are part of a special group of flycatchers that all look absolutely the same. They're officially called *Empidonax* flycatchers. The nerdiest of birdwatchers call them *empids*, and that makes my skin crawl. To make a confident identification, you'll need to note the bird's voice, behavior, and habitat.

Alder Flycatcher   

Willow Flycatcher  

In migration, these two can really only be separated by voice—or by flipping a coin. Just leave it up to chance. Or fu*ck it, pick whichever one you want it to be. This is your observation, your journey, your reality.

Acadian Flycatcher   

Song is affirmative, like it's spitting out a little checkmark. Again, you'll want to make sure you hear the bird before making any assumptions. The bird software police will prosecute you to the full extent of the law if you're proven incorrect.

Yellow-bellied Flycatcher   

We saw this one for the first time at a bird banding operation in Ohio. Some local scientists invited us to come watch one morning. *Bird banding* is when they catch birds in volleyball nets and then put them in bags. Later, they take them out of the bag, put a little ring on their leg, and let them go. They let us hold some of them too. Once a bird is released from your hand at the banding shed, the bird is both wild and unrestrained again—which means, if you watch it fly away, according to the rules put in place by the almighty ABA, you may count the observation on your lifer list.

Least Flycatcher   

Least, but certainly not last. Look for a bright white eyering. Once you find that, go ahead and remove your genitals—the fact that you can distinguish one grey bird from another almost identical grey bird clearly shows you'll no longer be needing them.

"They weren't heavy at all—I thought they would be heavy, like fish."
—Owen

Alder
Flycatcher
Willow
Flycatcher
Acadian
Flycatcher
Yellow-bellied
Flycatcher
Least
Flycatcher
scientist's
hand

Wacky World

Mississippi Kite

One of about a dozen birds we were lucky enough to catch in the act of mating—and the second type of kite.

Common Nighthawk

One of the best birds they've got around here. We both have deep memories of their calls during evening soccer practice growing up. They hunt around the lights because the lights attract bugs. We had no idea what it was when we were kids—and didn't even realize we had those memories until we started paying attention to birds. The sound of their wings when they dive is bonkers—it's like a cartoon race car.

Yellow-breasted Chat

Owen had a little yellow-breasted chat with his doctor—the rash is back. This bird is an entertaining mocker. We'd hear one near a marsh that would incorporate a kingfisher call into its song, or one near a field that would incorporate a quail call into its song. It's a wacky bird that can't really be lumped together with any other birds. It's simply too wacky.

Yellow-billed Cuckoo

These are long-tailed, kinda shy birds. They're fu*ckin cuckoo for Crazy Puffs, brother. They act how I'd be acting if I was a bird—just sneakin' around lookin' for weird bugs. This particular year was the first time since 1803 that both the thirteen-year (Brood XIX) and seventeen-year (Brood XIII) cicadas emerged simultaneously. Crazy Puffs must be made mostly of cicada parts—they absolutely love them.

Eastern Screech Owl

A man at the Magee Marsh boardwalk told us to come over to his scope because he *"had a treat for us."* With our a*ssholes puckered and our shivs ready, we obliged. Turned out he was just a nice guy, excited to share his owl sighting with us.

Mississippi
Kite
Common
Nighthawk
zooming
Brood XIX
Yellow-breasted
Chat
CRAAZY
PUFFS
Yellow-billed
Cuckoo
Eastern
Screech
Owl

Big Northwest

June & July

Duration: 59 days
Distance: 8,670mi
New Birds: 74
Total Birds: 498
Cracker Barrel Stays: 3

General Route: Southwest to Oklahoma, up through the Rocky Mountains, along the Gorge to Astoria, down the coast and inland as far as Corvallis, back up to Seattle, then back east through the Plains and down to Illinois.

Significant Places: Wichita Mountains WR, Glenrio Smoke Shop, Springer Lake, Carson NF, Twin Lakes, Leadville, Rocky Mountain NP, Lander, Yellowstone NP, Grand Teton NP, Missoula, Spokane, Yakima, Leavenworth, Liberty, Seattle, Olympic NF, Seaside, Saddle Mountain, Haystack Rock, Corvallis, Harlowton, Old Gap Road, Amidon, Sax-Zim Bog.

Weather: Variable

Overview

This was our longest and toughest trip. Great fun was had, and many birds were found, but two months on the road does wear you down. We traveled through some of the best and most rugged landscapes this country has to offer. At points, we pushed the minivan a little too hard. We ended up having to patch a couple of flat tires. By the time we got back home, the brakes were toast, the axle was snapped, and the windshield was cracked. But we made it back.

We were focused on people during this trip a little more than on our previous ones. Somewhere along the way, we decided we were turning our quest into a movie, so we ended up interviewing anyone who was willing. Many people also reached out to us and offered tips, food, drugs, and places to sleep. You know who you are, and you should know that we are forever grateful.

By this time, I'd woken up from the pipe dream that we were going to see every single bird that enters the country—but we learned that someone else was attempting that. The Ivy League bird software has a leaderboard, and at the top sat a 19-year-old kid with over a hundred more birds on his list than ours. Holy smokes, bud. He would end up breaking the record for most birds seen in one year in the Lower 48. The winner of the Big Year doesn't get any money or trophies— just bragging rights.

We obviously didn't have the drive or the skills to compete with someone like this, but I think we can say that no one has seen more bird species in one year—while living out of a Kia Sedona minivan—than Owen and I.

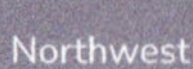

Oklahoma

 Oklahoma is pretty much just a turnpike. Every time you drive through their dusty-a*ss state, they send you a bill for $30. One bright spot is the Wichita Mountains, where we saw these birds.

Painted Bunting

As if a kindergarten teacher asked her students to design a bird.

Cave Swallow

I'll never forget my *lifer*.

Black-capped Vireo

This bird wears a hockey helmet. This bird is a menace. This bird is a fourth-line grinder, not afraid to mix it up. This bird is a greaseball—it slap shots on empty netters. You hate to play against this bird, but you'd love to have it on your team.

Scissor-tailed Flycatcher

Scissor me timbers, what a tail. In summer, they line the fences and electrical wires all over Oklahoma and Texas.

Dispensary

There's a dispensary in Glenrio, New Mexico—on the state line. It's the best dispensary I've been to, and also a great birding spot

Scaled Quail

Down the road from the dispensary, we observed a single bird perched and singing in a dead tree next to a decrepit old building with the words *"modern restrooms"* painted on the side.

Bullock's Oriole

In the dispensary parking lot, we saw a bright orange and black bird fly in and post up in a tree. We tried to call it in with electronic dance music.

Sage Thrasher

Just thrashin' sage, and bottlin' up rage.

Painted
Bunting
m.
Cave
Swallow
Black-capped
Vireo
m.
Scissor-tailed
Flycatcher
tail
in
flight
Scaled
Quail
Bullock's
Oriole
m.
dispensary
Sage Thrasher

Rocky Mountain High

Williamson's Sapsucker   

The male is striking, apparently. We only saw a female, and that's okay—I'm not mad about it. Makes a horrible, horrible noise.

Clark's Nutcracker  

Sort of a middle ground between a jay and a woodpecker. Makes a horrible, horrible noise.

Cassin's Finch   

Mountain House Finch. See: House Finch, Purple Finch.

Pine Grosbeak   

Not the sharpest of the grosbeaks. I think they kind of slipped up on this one, to be honest.

Black-headed Grosbeak   

Saw one at a nice campground in the mountains of northern New Mexico, near a beautiful creek. We thought, ahh, fu*ck it—we'll pay for a night, it's only $8. All we had was change, so I filled one of their envelopes with quarters and dimes and tried to jam it into the metal fee pipe, but it wouldn't fit. The large campground host saw me struggling and waddled over. I figured I could just pay him. I was wrong. He rudely explained that we couldn't camp there without a reservation through Rec.gov, even though the whole place was empty. Filling out forms on an awful website and paying *admin* fees just didn't sound that fun, so we left and camped elsewhere for free. That's the name of the game.

Plumbeous Vireo   

Plumbeous means grey. This is a grey bird. Similar to a couple other vireos. See Cassin's & Blue-Headed Vireo.

Mountain Bluebird   

Of the three species of bluebirds we saw, this one's the bluest.

White-tailed Ptarmigan   

We saw a pair at the ptippy ptop of a mountain.

Williamson's
Sapsucker
f.
Clark's
Nutcracker
Pine
Grosbeak
m.
Cassin's
Finch
m.
m.
Plumbeous
Vireo
Black-headed
Grosbeak
White-tailed
Ptarmigan
Mountain
Bluebird
m.
m.

But Wait, There's More

If you thought flycatchers got any easier out west, you'd be wrong. There's a whole new gang of prima donnas waiting for you to misidentify.

Dusky Flycatcher

An older man once told us to remember that *"Dusky never dips"*—meaning, it doesn't dip or wag its tail downward like some of the other prima donnas.

Western Flycatcher

This one is easier—damn near conspicuous. They look a little more greenish-yellow if you happen to have perfect lighting conditions.

Hammond's Flycatcher

The same older man also told us that *"Hammond's hangs high"*— meaning, it's more likely to be perched high in the trees. They also flick their wings and tail out, which can give you a clue.

Western Wood Pewee

This one's not a prima donna, but it fooled us more than once. Compared to the Eastern Wood Pewee, the Western is a little more of a greaser. See: Eastern Wood Pewee.

Tuna Rice Recipe

1 onion
2 jalapeños
2 cups instant rice + appropriate amount of water
2 cans albacore tuna in EVOO
1 avocado
1 tbsp EVOO
salt, garlic powder, chili powder (to taste)

Directions:
Scrape out last night's tuna rice. Dice onion and jalapeño, and sauté in EVOO. Add water and bring to a boil. Add rice and seasonings. Stir, cover, and remove from heat. Let the rice swell until no water remains. Add tuna. Put half in a bowl for your brother. Top with avocado and hot sauce.

Dusky Flycatcher
Western Flycatcher
Western Wood Pewee
Hammond's Flycatcher
wing/tail flick

Maven Optics

 In the springtime, an optics company contacted us and sent us a pair of binoculars. They were made of plastic and fell apart in a couple months. We appreciated the generosity, but not the quality. In the summer, **Maven Optics**—a company out of **Lander, Wyoming**—called us up to the big leagues. The folks at Maven invited us to tour their facility—and then gave us a bunch of big boy optics. Everyone there was strong, tough, and handsome. They all love the outdoors and are passionate about hunting and conservation. Some of them don't even mind birdwatching. They didn't threaten us or make us say any of this—we genuinely believe they make great optics. They filled our bellies, put us up in a motel for the night, and then told us to get the he*ck out there and find the birds depicted here. We found them all—because **Maven Optics** are good.

Greater Sage Grouse

 You can find them out in the sagebrush, as you might assume. In the sagebrush outside of town we came across a semi truck parked in the middle of the road, blocking our turn. As I weaseled around it, what came into view was a truck driver with his pants down, halfway squatting in the road while white-knuckling the door handle. Listen—we love our truckers. We *need* our truckers in America. But we need our truckers to be *driving*, not painting the concrete with undigested Arby's.

California Gull

We saw more of these seagulls on dry land than in any body of water.

Sagebrush Sparrow

Very dry bird. I'd imagine the meat is pretty tough and stringy. Plumage is similar to that of the Bell's Sparrow, but the two species can be separated by voice and range. See: Bell's Sparrow.

Mountain Plover

What did the police officer say to the shorebird that was running away?
Plover.

Greater
Sage Grouse
m.
B1.2 / 8x42
S3 / 20-40x67
California
Gull
B1.2 / 8x42
Sagebrush
Sparrow
Mountain
Plover
B.3 / 10x30

Upper Mountain West

Cassin's Vireo

Similar to a couple other vireos. See: Blue-headed & Plumbeous Vireo.

Black-throated Grey Warbler

This sighting completed our triple crown of Black-throated warblers. See: Black-throated Blue & Black-throated Green Warbler.

MacGillivray's Warbler

MacGiveItToMe Warbler.

Clark's Grebe

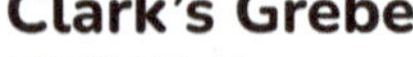 If you want to find a Clark's Grebe, you'll need to go to an all-women's prison. When you get there, look for a lake behind the prison. Sleep in your van with your brother at the lake. In the morning, listen to 2009 pop hits. If you did all that correctly, the bird will be out in the water, ready to be viewed.

Red-necked Grebe

Saw a few just north of Missoula, MT. Missoula's a great place, but there is a man there who will kill me if he finds out I'm around.

Barrow's Goldeneye

Just north of Jackson Hole—a place you should try to avoid— we saw a single female hanging out in Flat Creek.

American Dipper

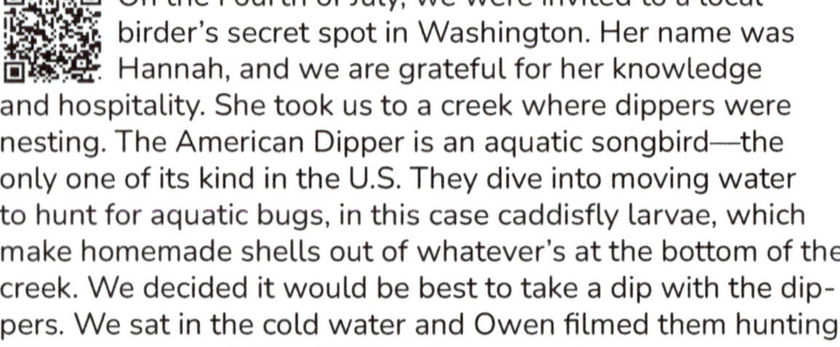 On the Fourth of July, we were invited to a local birder's secret spot in Washington. Her name was Hannah, and we are grateful for her knowledge and hospitality. She took us to a creek where dippers were nesting. The American Dipper is an aquatic songbird—the only one of its kind in the U.S. They dive into moving water to hunt for aquatic bugs, in this case caddisfly larvae, which make homemade shells out of whatever's at the bottom of the creek. We decided it would be best to take a dip with the dip-pers. We sat in the cold water and Owen filmed them hunting. When we got out, I had 23 leeches on my leg.

Cassin's Vireo
Black-throated Grey Warbler
m.
MacGillivray's Warbler
m.
Red-necked Grebe
br.
Clark's Grebe
Barrow's Goldeneye
f.
American Dipper
caddisfly larva

PNW Forest

The forests of the Pacific Northwest are beautiful, eerie, and magical places. While we were up there, we spent most of our forest time in coastal Oregon looking for the local birds. Oregon is a beautiful place, but it's also a huge dump. It was a struggle to find free camping because most access to state forests had recently been closed due to a bunch of bums dumping large amounts of trash in them. Thanks, guys.

Band-tailed Pigeon

A native forest pigeon—a nice changeup from the more wide-spread, city-dwelling Rock Pigeon. See: Rock Pigeon.

Townsend's Warbler

Sharply-patterned black and yellow warbler.

Hermit Warbler

At the location we saw this little yellow-headed home boy, I stepped in human shi*t. I love Oregon.

Varied Thrush

High-pitched, eerie song that rings through the forest. Just a single, long note at a time that can give you chills. They can be hard to find in the huge trees, but they're worth a look. The most strikingly patterned thrush you'll find in this book.

Red-breasted Sapsucker

This bird would complete our grand slam of sapsuckers. By far the hardest one for us to find—even sneakier than the rest.

Chestnut-backed Chickadee

Chickadees are just some of the boys.

Pacific Wren

 Like most of the other wrens we found, it has a very musical and chaotic song. Around the same time we found this one, we also came across a dead dog someone had dumped off a forest service road. Isn't Oregon lovely?

Band-tailed Pigeon
Townsend's Warbler
m.
Varied Thrush
Hermit Warbler
m.
Chestnut-backed Chickadee
Red-breasted Sapsucker
m.
Pacific Wren

Oregon Coast

Pacific Loon

Crisply patterned loon, with a hunched posture in-flight. We got great looks at one through our new Maven scope. See: Maven Optics.

Red-throated Loon

 This loon also has a hunched back in flight. We didn't get a great look at it—given it was a quarter mile out over the ocean on a cloudy day. We did, however, get good looks at a couple other loons in a Safeway parking lot.

Brandt's Cormorant

These are large cormorants. They have a sort of turquoise eyeball.

Pelagic Cormorant

These are small cormorants. We were able to tell them apart easily from the other nearby cormorants by the large white patches they sport behind their wings during the breeding season. We observed them building and occupying nests on the sea stacks.

White-winged Scoter

A dark sea duck. The males and females both have white patches on the trailing edge of the wings.

Rhinoceros Auklet

Plump little seabird that flies like a football with tiny wings.

"They say there are more stars in the universe than grains of sand on Earth—
*but I think they forgot to count the ones in my a*ss crack."*
—Owen

Pacific
Loon
Red-throated
Loon
Brandt's Cormorant
Pelagic
Cormorant
nesting
m.
White-winged
Scoter
Rhinoceros
Auklet

Haystack Rock

 Haystack Rock is a sea stack—a giant rock on the edge of the beach that you can walk up to at low tide. The rock is covered in birds, bird shi*t, barnacles, mussels, and starfish. While we were there, we met an Australian bloke who'd been mad enough to cycle 3,500 *kilometers* up the West Coast and casually tally 248 species of bird along the way. His name was Fred, and these are the birds we saw with him.

Common Murre

This was probably the most exotic bird we'd heard about before this whole thing started. A few years back, while we were driving up the 101 in Oregon one night, Owen accidentally obliterated a *"penguin"* on the road, and we tried to identify it later on Google dot com. There were hundreds on this rock.

Tufted Puffin

*"Where is the bloody cu*nt? What a glorious ba*stard"* - Fred

Glaucous-winged Gull

To pick out one of these seagulls from the other, more common seagulls, pay special attention to the color of the wingtips. The wingtips of the Glaucous-winged Gull are light grey—same color as the rest of the wing. The other nearby seagulls (Western, Herring) have black wingtips that contrast with the rest of the wing. See Western & Herring Gull.

Pigeon Guillemot

A pigeon and a puffin fell in love.

Harlequin Duck

These ducks are seemingly unfazed by the violent crashing and slushing of waves and whitewater in the areas they occupy most frequently. Danger is their middle name. Harlequin *Danger* Duck.

Black Oystercatcher

Similar to the American Oystercatcher in the Southeast, but this one is all dark. I like this one more, but again—catching an oyster is not that impressive. See: American Oystercatcher.

Common
Murre
those things
in my eye
Tufted
Puffin
Glaucous-winged
Gull
Pigeon
Guillemot
Harlequin
Duck
Black
Oystercatcher

Coupla Swifts & Hummers

You likely wont get a very long stable look at any of these birds—they're usually on the move.

Vaux's Swift

It's pretty much just like a Chimney Swift—they use chimneys to roost and nest as well. Every birder we asked said it was pronounced *"vox,"* not *"voh"*—because we're in America. It got me thinking about how the French really fu*cked up on the Louisiana Purchase. Those snobs got absolutely hosed. This place is unreal. See: Chimney Swift.

Black Swift

This Swift programming language made me thousands of dollars over the past decade, but this bird on the other hand, didn't make me a dime. It actually cost me money.

Calliope Hummingbird

Pretty high altitude hummingbird, we thought.

Broad-tailed Hummingbird

After my come-to-Jesus moment on the marijuana edible during spring migration, I settled down and didn't get too mad about missing a bird or failing to get a good photo to upload to the bird database. But that's not to say I didn't have my aftershocks. One of those times was with this hummingbird. We kept hearing them and seeing them whiz by, but I just couldn't snap a good photo. Trying to dial in a manual focus ring while aiming at a tiny moving target can be quite difficult. I was getting pi*ssed, but I remembered my past. I gave up on getting a good shot—because *who cares, dude?* There's nothing serious about any of this. I present to you my best image of this hummingbird.

Rufous Hummingbird

This is a small orange bird.

"Yeah, no, I saw it fly by. The orange, yeah, it was orange."
—Owen

Vaux's
Swift
Black
Swift
Calliope
Hummingbird
m.
m.
Rufous
Hummingbird
m.
Broad-tailed
Hummingbird

Northwest Killers

Ferruginous Hawk

This is the biggest hawk they make. We watched one eat a prairie dog atop a wooden pole. *Ferruginous* is another way to say brown. *Brown Hawk* just doesn't have quite the same ring to it. The one depicted here is a dark morph.

Peregrine Falcon

A super fu*cking fast animal. Apparently the fastest one they make.

Golden Eagle

Massive flying animal that demands your attention. Scarier than the Bald Eagle by a country mile. See: Bald Eagle.

Owl Boys

A couple nice young lads offered to take us out owling near Liberty, Washington. We were a little hesitant after our spooky encounter with the big cat while owling in Arizona, but we ended up taking their offer. The boys picked us up in their SUV and we ripped up and down forest service roads through the night.

Northern Pygmy Owl

 On this trip, Owen brought a harmonica and I brought a recorder—a plastic flute, basically. I figured out how to imitate a Northern Pygmy Owl with it well enough to fool the Ivy League bird software, so I gave it a shot. I spent an evening playing the flute in the woods while wearing binoculars, pink sunglasses, and sandals. My performance was unsuccessful. A few days later, the owl kids called one in by whistling. Professionals.

Flammulated Owl

The kids call them *flammies*.

Northern Saw-whet Owl

We got the best looks at this one. The kids shined a flashlight on it, which does feel a bit intrusive, but man, that thing was nice.

Ferruginous
Hawk
dark
morph
Peregrine
Falcon
Golden
Eagle
Northern
Pygmy-Owl
Northern
Saw-whet Owl
Flammulated
Owl

Dry Field

Ring-necked Pheasant

At the spot we saw these introduced pheasants, we met a man with a huge camera lens and an owl tattoo who kept telling us he wasn't *really* a birder. Sure, dude—and I'm not *really* evading the IRS.

Thick-billed Longspur

Chestnut-collared Longspur

Longspurs are just fancy sparrows. When you're out driving the dirt roads, and a farmer rolls by and asks if you're lost, tell him you're just birdwatching—but say you're looking for something more socially acceptable, like an eagle or a falcon.

Grey Partridge

 They must have been running 30 miles per every one hour when we saw them. They're a stout terrestrial bird that can run fast as shi*t. We were deep into the year but still relying heavily on the text to identify birds. It was our first time ever seeing any of them. Six months prior, I thought a partridge was just a dumpy Christmas ornament.

Upland Sandpiper

Large shorebird, usually nowhere near the shore. They're out in the field there. Big fans of those wooden posts.

Chukar

 On the world's hottest day, next to a large dead deer, is where we saw these introduced partridges. They're the national bird of Pakistan, but they feel right at home in central Washington, where the weather is just as brutal.

Sprague's Pipit

The juvenile Horned Lark looks very similar to this pipit. We mistook one of the young larks for one of these birds and reported it on the bird software. The authorities were on us almost immediately. We learned from our mistake and found the correct birds the following day.

Ring-necked
Pheasant
m.
Thick-billed
Longspur
m.
Grey
Partridge
m.
Chestnut-collared
Longspur
Upland
Sandpiper
Chukar
Sprague's
Pipit

Wet Field

Clay-colored Sparrow

Clay comes in many colors—so yeah, of course it is.

Sharp-tailed Grouse

We watched a couple of these grice dirt-bathe in the road from a great distance.

Bobolink

Robert O. Link

Baird's Sparrow

A sought-after sparrow, for some reason. Birding takes you to the strangest places. The only reason you'd ever be in Amidon, North Dakota is to check your rapeseed field—or to find this very specific sparrow.

LeConte's Sparrow

Very boldly patterned sparrow. If it weren't so French, I'd say I like it.

Yellow Rail

 A small marsh chicken a little bigger than a sparrow, it's rarely seen unless you go to one of those events where they mow the habitat down until one is forced to fly out. We did not bring a mower with us on our two-month trip. What someone told us to try, though, was taking two rocks and tapping them together to imitate the bird's song—a clicking noise. As two recovering playback users, we were eager to try it, and to our surprise, it worked. We found a nearby sighting report on the bird software and hung around the area one night. Right around 10 p.m., on a gravel farm road, covered from head to toe in mosquito-proof clothing and drenched in sweat, we got to hear a small, shy bird.

Virginia Rail

Another marsh chicken. Not quite as shy, but they do prefer to be out of sight.

Clay-colored
Sparrow
Sharp-tailed
Grouse
Bobolink
Baird's
Sparrow
LeConte's
Sparrow
ClicK
ClicK
ClicK
rock
tapping
Virginia
Rail
Yellow
Rail

Southwest II

Mid August - Late September

Duration: 49 days
Distance: 7,722mi
New Birds: 57
Total Birds: 555
Cracker Barrel Stays: 2

General Route: I-70 west to Colorado, south to Los Alamos and Las Cruces, west to Arizona, north to Flagstaff, over to Las Vegas, Death Valley, Bakersfield, and San Francisco, then south to Oceanside—avoiding LA—back east to southeast Arizona, north to Flagstaff, and I-40 east back to Illinois.

Significant Places: Los Alamos, Bandelier NM, Santa Fe Ski Hill, Chiricahuas, Santa Ritas, Patagonia, Nogales, Tucson, Donna R. Liggens Center, Grand Canyon, Las Vegas, Bakersfield, San Francisco, Half Moon Bay, the Pacific Ocean, Channel Islands NP, Pinnacles NP, Oceanside.

Weather: Hotter than a witch's titty.

Overview

 After the big northwest trip, we were starting to grow a little tired of this whole thing. We were in the dog days of summer, and new birds were becoming increasingly difficult to find. During the two weeks we spent at home, we did all the necessary maintenance to make the van bird-worthy again. We also got our a*sses kicked in the national roller hockey tournament. No worries.

The centerpiece of this trip was the pelagic boat outing we willingly signed up for, but there were also a decent number of birds we'd missed on our previous trip out there. We didn't need much of an excuse to go back to Arizona, but post-monsoon season is a great time to be there. We'd end up spending more time in the southeastern part of the state, since we enjoyed it so much previously. We also went down into the Grand Canyon two separate times. One of those times, we went with some friends, and one of them brought a British woman along for some reason. She, of course, shat her trousers at the bottom and stunk up the whole canyon. Now I wasn't sure who was worse—the French or the British. But this is beside the point.

It was much hotter, which made sleeping in the van uncomfortable. Our bodies adapted, and we persisted. For the love of the game.

The Reward

Grey Flycatcher

We saw this bird near Los Alamos National Labs—the place that makes efficient methods for killing people. This bird wags its tail.

American Three-toed Woodpecker

 We agreed to help a couple of master's students with their fieldwork in Bandelier, NM. Our job: haul 70 lbs of water each a few miles out into the desert in 110-degree heat. Our payment: eating unsalted beans under a juniper tree. When I asked if they brought enough salt, they said they didn't bring any—I guess they don't teach that in master's school. Owen and I left at 3 a.m. the next morning to beat the heat. We figured the students would all be found dead in a couple days from the salt deficiency, but we were on our way back with the directions they gave us for the *"short way."* The short way involved steep grade, loose rock, and heavy vegetation—in the dark. Just when we thought it couldn't get worse, we were sprayed by a skunk. When we made it out, we went straight to the Santa Fe ski hill for a break from the heat. We spent the day eating THC sweet tarts and fu*cking off. I was taking a nap when I woke up to Owen, high as a kite, sitting outside the van mumbling, *"Woodpecker."* Much to our surprise, it was the American Three-toed Woodpecker—a bird we'd been chasing for months all across the West. Turns out, all we had to do was get loaded at the top of a ski hill.

Buff-breasted Flycatcher

Owen thought I was an insane man when I abruptly stopped the van, flung open the door, and ran out after this little prima donna.

Botteri's Sparrow

"I'm gonna be honest, I don't remember that one." —Owen

Varied Bunting

Not a super common bird—a real treat to get glass on this one.

Juniper Titmouse

Call it a Jupiter Titmouse—because it's out of this world.

Grey
Flycatcher
American
Three-toed
Woodpecker
tail
wag
sweet
tarts
2mg
Buff-breasted
Flycatcher
Botteri's
Sparrow
Varied
Bunting
m.
Juniper
Titmouse

Flycatcher City

 We were back for another stint in Patagonia. This time, we were after flycatchers—and they were buzzing. Patagonia is one of the places of the year. What a place that place is. It's quiet, and no one drives too fast, and if you know one Spanish word, you can get a huge bag of dates for five bucks. You can sleep for free near a mining operation, and in the morning, you can wake up to exotic birds outside your minivan.

Rose-throated Becard

These birds are considered rare in the United States, but a few pairs breed within the states every year—like this one attempted to do. This bird, a female who does not wear the namesake rose throat, built a nest but never found a suitable mate. A sad story for such a nice bird. We waited at the site for hours, dippin' our feet in the creek and admiring the flashy grasshoppers nearby. I stepped away to relieve myself, and that's when Owen spotted the bird.

Thick-billed Kingbird

The bill was so thick that I started to get emotional, and vaguely religious.

Northern Beardless Tyrannulet

Super big name for a super small bird.

Sulphur-bellied Flycatcher

Sometimes I'll eat too many eggs at once and get a bit of a sulfur belly myself. It's quite remarkably patterned—dark above and yellowish below. Bold white mustache and headpiece. A reddish-orange tail. Fine streaking throughout. Its voice sounds just like a squeaky toy.

Brown-crested Flycatcher

This bird was rather elusive. Looks very similar to other flycatchers that you can see in the same place. See: Ash-throated & Dusky-capped Flycatcher.

Rose-throated
Becard
f.
Thick-billed
Kingbird
Northern
Beardless
Tyrannulet
Sulphur-bellied
Flycatcher
Brown-crested
Flycatcher

California For Real

It was time to go to California for real this time. Earlier in the year, we'd poked in for a few days just to pick up our buddy and buzz on out. This time, we'd do it properly. There were a decent number of birds left on the table in California, and we had to make it to Half Moon Bay for our pelagic boat trip. It's always been a love-hate relationship with California. It's arguably the most beautiful state, but there are some major drawbacks. In California, everything is more expensive, there are a bajillion people, and it seems like a lot of them don't want you to be there. We prepared to have a terrible time while we were there. We mentally prepared to have something go wrong with the van or have all of our stuff stolen—but luckily, this would not be the case.

White-headed Woodpecker  

"Looks better in the guidebook than in real life." —Sparky

Slate-throated Redstart   

The morning after boondocking at the rest stop north of the Golden Gate Bridge, we headed into the heart of San Francisco. We stopped at a drugstore to pick up meds for the pelagic. In the parking lot, we met a foreign woman who was picking up cigarette butts to upcycle. We helped point some out to her, and she thought we were funny for doing so. We also met a man who gave us each a pastry because he'd made too many. Maybe this place wasn't so bad after all. Next, we went to a park to search for this very rare bird. We followed a group of birders around and documented the chase. When they found it, one guy farted just out of excitement. Others were calling loved ones to tell them about the find. Owen and I saw the bird briefly. It was a grey and red smudge, obscured by sticks and leaves.

Scaly-breasted Munia   

Chestnut above, very scaly below. Non-native, but that's okay.

Bell's Sparrow 

Likes it hot and dry.

Ridgway's Rail  

Loves a good lagoon.

White-headed
Woodpecker
m.
Slate-throated
Redstart
m.
Scaly-breasted
Munia
Bell's
Sparrow
Ridgway's
Rail

Show Me The Way To Go Home

 Pelagic birding is the final frontier. It's where the most passionate birders pile into a small boat and travel 40 miles or more out to sea for the chance to glimpse seabirds—often just silhouettes trailing the water far off in the distance, or small, dark lumps floating on the waves.

The night before our pelagic trip, Owen and I camped in a dark corner of the Half Moon Bay Marina parking lot. Since neither of us had been on a boat out to sea, we concocted a small scientific experiment for the journey. Owen would take the recommended dose of generic motion sickness meds. I'd be the control group and take a small dose of psilocybin mushrooms. This would result in several significant findings.

The next morning, aboard the *New Captain Pete*, under the guidance of our fearless leader **Alvaro**, the first few hours were tolerable—uncomfortable, but manageable. We held down a corner at the back of the boat where we could wedge ourselves against the railing and remain relatively stable. As first-timers, we'd been told to stick to the back if we were worried about seasickness. The spotters on board called out every bird, gave identification tips, and answered all our stupid questions.

Eventually, breathing the exhaust at the back of the boat—coupled with the constant, unpredictable movement and the psychedelics—required that my body evacuate the contents of the stomach, which happened nine times. Hydration was impossible. Every time I took a drink of water, it was rejected. Time was direction, the compass was a British man, everything was wet, and the whales were trying to speak to us. When I closed my eyes, I saw stacks of disks floating above one another, each wobbling out of sync. I realized I'd never reach equilibrium, and just had to accept my state of being a wobbly piece of jerky lost at sea. But despite my condition, I managed to stay in a good mood for the entirety of the trip. I stayed upright the whole time, which is more than Owen can say. I'm not really selling it well, but if you ever decide to take a pelagic birding tour, it better be with *Alvaro's Adventures.*

Arctic Tern

Pomarine Jaeger

Parasitic Jaeger

Long-tailed Jaeger

South Polar Skua

Jaegers and skuas are bullies. They chase other birds until they give up—or throw up—their food. Didn't have to chase me.

Cocos Booby

Black-footed Albatross

9 o'clock, above horizon.

Sabine's Gull

Not bad for a seagull.

Ashy Storm Petrel

Buller's Shearwater

Pink-footed Shearwater

Sooty Shearwater

Shi*tty Sewerwater.

Scripps's Murrelet

Marbled Murrelet

Guadalupe Murrelet

As everyone rushed to one side of the boat to watch a tiny dot in the sea, I watched Owen lie down on the bench and quietly pass out—he had the foresight to get horizontal first. The rare Guadalupe Murrelet was just too much for him. When he came to, I was lightly smacking his face while Alvaro stood nearby, defibrillator in hand. Someone handed him a pill and a Gatorade. He was fine—bent, really bent, but not broken.

Cassin's Auklet

Red Phalarope

Northern Fulmar

Arctic Tern
Pomarine Jaeger
Cocos Booby
South Polar Skua
Buller's Shearwater
Pink-footed Shearwater
Sooty Shearwater
Scripps's Murrelet
Marbled Murrelet
Cassin's Auklet
Guadalupe Murrelet

Parasitic Jaeger
Long-tailed Jaeger
Black-footed Albatross
Sabine's Gull
Ashy Storm Petrel
Red Phalarope
Northern Fulmar

Oh No, Not Again

Red-necked Phalarope

Wilson's Phalarope

Owen thought these were called *"Thalaropes"* for several weeks. He'd never seen it written. Both of these species spin around in shallow water to stir up shi*t to eat. Based on our research, there's no obvious preference for clockwise or counterclockwise.

Island Scrub Jay

I didn't think we'd ever get on a boat again, but just four days after our traumatic time out to sea, we were heading to Santa Cruz Island for the chance to see the endemic Island Scrub Jay. A man named Jeremy, who works on the island, contacted us and said he had two free ferry tickets for us. He offered to take us sea kayaking as well. How could we pass this up? I was in, but it took some effort to convince Owen. The boat was much bigger, and the ride was only an hour. Owen did not lose consciousness, and I held onto all the contents of my stomach. On board the ferry, we met a man who kept telling us he was famous for singing the Coca-Cola theme song in commercials. He gave us each a cookie. No worries. On the island, we saw the bird we were after within five minutes. We spent the rest of the time sea kayaking with Jeremy and a Navy SEAL who thought he was back in boot camp.

Black-vented Shearwater

Pointed out to us by the captain of the ferry.

Elegant Tern

Nothing elegant about squirting fish juice out of your cloaca.

Wandering Tattler

Traveling Snitch.

Black Turnstone

Cousin to the Ruddy Turnstone. See: Ruddy Turnstone.

Surfbird

Get pitted, brah.

Red-necked
Phalarope
nb./im.
Wilson's
Phalarope
j.
Island
Scrub Jay
Black-vented
Shearwater
Elegant
Tern
br.
Wandering
Tattler
nb.
Surfbird
nb.
Black
Turnstone
nb.

Dry Guys

California Condor

 This is essentially a massive Turkey Vulture. When I was six years old, I decided this was my favorite bird because it was the biggest one I could find in the guidebook. Twenty-three years later, it's not my favorite bird anymore—but it's alright. California Condors nearly went extinct from ingesting too much DMT and lead shot, or something like that. Humans nearly wiped them out, but then they saved them. Now they're doin' alright. Almost all of them are tagged with a number on one or both of their wings. If you get a good enough look at the tag, you can look up the bird's stat page online. The particular individual we saw at Pinnacles National Park wears tag number 88 and goes by the human name *Cedric*. See: Turkey Vulture.

California Thrasher

 It's *my* lifer, and no one's ever gonna take it away from me. We drove through the mountains in the dark for hours on our way to a campsite. They were doing construction on the windy, two-lane road, so they had automatic timed red lights set up for miles. Not a soul out there—just us, letting these machines dictate our lives. We kept getting stuck at them, delaying our much-needed bedtime. When we finally arrived at the National Forest, the access was closed. So we just opted for a pull-off next to the road. The rest is history.

Yellow-billed Magpie

This bird had some gnarly growth on its eye.

California Quail

For fu*ck's sake, all these California birds again. *"Oh, we've got our own quail too!"*

Mountain Quail

We got lucky with these. We were driving up into the mountains of the Eldorado National Forest to find a place to camp and came across a group of mostly immature birds crossing the road. This sighting completed our quail quintet for the year.

California
Condor
m.
tag
88
not
to scale
California
Thrasher
Yellow-billed
Magpie
m.
im.
Mountain
Quail
California
Quail

Back To Arizona

Plain-capped Starthroat

 This is a greenish hummingbird with a white mustache, a white eyebrow, and a small white patch on its back. The sexes are similar. We eventually made our way back to the promised land of Arizona and found ourselves camping on Proctor Road at the base of the Santa Ritas. It's beautiful there—easily one of the top campsites of the year. Just us, the sparrows, and the cows. We had plans to summit Mt. Wrightson in the morning, so we were just resting up and enjoying the views after dinner. That's when we checked the rare bird reports and saw this hummingbird had been reported just up the road at Santa Rita Lodge—a place where old folks watch hummingbirds drink sugar water. Nothing wrong with it—it's awesome—it just has more of a petting zoo vibe and almost feels like you're cheating the game. In the morning, we finished our hike and buzzed back down to the lodge, where we learned that the kid who'd end up breaking the record for most birds seen in a year had already come and gone. He'd driven 18 hours straight to add this one to his list. We had no idea the night before—we just happened to be camping in the right spot. The bird gods were definitely on our side. You do sometimes get into interesting conversations at feeders. While we waited for the bird, we talked to a snake guy. He had a ponytail—like all snake guys—and told us he'd been bitten by rattlesnakes on eight different occasions.

Berylline Hummingbird

Berylline is French for bluish-green.

Mexican Whip-poor-will

Named this way because of the sound it makes—a repetitive *whip-poor-will*, trilled or rolled like an "r" in Spanish.

Lesser Nighthawk

Not quite the same. See: Common Nighthawk.

Western Screech Owl

A small, murderous tooter.

Plain-capped
Starthroat

Berylline
Hummingbird

Mexican
Whip-poor-will

Lesser
Nighthawk

Western
Screech Owl

So Long Southwest

If I could only choose one state to birdwatch in, it'd be Arizona. By far the most time we spent in any single state. It's not just the variety of birds—it's the landscape, the access to good food, the free camping, the peace and quiet. It's the whole package. Wrapping things up was bittersweet. It was still a hundred degrees at this time, so leaving that behind was okay—but knowing we wouldn't be coming back for the rest of the year gave us pause. We reflected on our time spent there. Arizona is a place we'd been going to for years, but this year was the first time we'd truly gotten to know it—thanks to birdwatching, of all things.

Grace's Warbler

Right where we saw this bird, we met an older man wearing incredibly short shorts. He spoke gracefully about dragonflies while we maintained eye contact.

Olive Warbler

A Tucson birder showed us this bird near the top of Mt. Lemmon, where he also cleaned shi*t off his dog's a*ss and legs.

Mexican Chickadee

Chickadees are just some of the niños.

Red-faced Warbler

Clearly has a drinking problem.

Canyon Wren

 We ended our tenure in Arizona for the year the best way we know how—doing a Rim2Rim2Rim of the Grand Canyon, of course. We left the South Rim at midnight and made it to the North Rim and back before sunset. Over the course of 46 miles, Owen got a chafed scrotum, and I ate a full jar of mayonnaise. The best iced tea in the world is at Phantom Ranch, at the bottom of the canyon. We saw many birds, but none more appropriate than the Canyon Wren. Their song descending down the walls of the canyon is something special, and best experienced in the biggest canyon they got. We saw or heard eleven individuals across our trek. By my rough estimates, you could fit over 60 quadrillion Canyon Wrens in the Grand Canyon.

Grace's Warbler
m.
Olive Warbler
f.
Red-faced Warbler
m.
Mexican Chickadee
Canyon Wren
song
anti-chafing application

Florida & Texas II

Mid October - Mid November

Duration: 27 days
Distance: 5,493mi
New Birds: 19
Total Birds: 574
Cracker Barrel Stays: 11

General Route: South to Nashville, then Pensacola, down the coast to Miami, Homestead, the Everglades, then out to the Keys. Continued along the coast to Biloxi, then farther west to the RGV, before heading back north through Louisiana and Arkansas.

Significant Places: Nashville, Fort Myers, Homestead, Miami, Everglades NP, Florida Bay, the Keys, Biloxi, Bolivar Flats, Corpus Christi, the RGV.

Weather: Hot and humid. Not the slightest bit comfortable.

Overview

This trip started off with a wedding in Nashville. We'd already dodged two weddings earlier in the year, but we had to be in the wedding party for this one. They make you pay for your own suit—can you believe that? This meant we didn't have money to put toward a nice hotel room, which meant we'd be the only ones in the wedding party spending two nights, slightly buzzed, in a Cracker Barrel parking lot.

Doing a big year means you're very busy doing something very unimportant. It might be important to you, but in the grand scheme of things, it's a silly endeavor. In our case, we hadn't had an interest in birds at all before the quest, so our friends and family didn't understand what we were doing or why we were doing it—and that's okay, neither did we. I basically blacked out for an entire year and woke up with a list of animals and a huge credit card bill. No worries.

This would be our last long trip, and we'd pretty much run it back with the original Florida and Texas route. There weren't that many new birds left for us to see—but that just meant we'd already seen a fu*ck ton. The second outing to Florida confirmed that it's the toughest state to live out of a minivan in. The second outing to Texas confirmed that it's the second toughest state to live out of a minivan in.

The Keys To Our Dreams

The Florida Keys are hot and humid. They're home to the oldest, wrinkliest people you'll likely ever see. It's a long drive out to the westernmost key, and for us it wasn't quite worth it. Most of the cool migrants, like the Swallow-tailed Kite, and the Antillean Nighthawk, were farther south by this time, so we'd miss out on those. We did enjoy the frigatebirds though.

White-crowned Pigeon 

Should be renamed *Bald Pigeon* for consistency.

Magnificent Frigatebird 

Magnificent friggin' bird.

Clapper Rail 

I barely know her rail.

No See Ems

No-see-ums are maybe some of the most evil work put out by Mother Nature—teeny tiny little biting flies that travel around in swarms of trillions, it seems like. You've really gotta stay covered at all times near any body of water. While we were being eaten alive, we added a couple more no-see-um tallies to our list.

Mitred Parakeet 

We did actually see this one—but so briefly, we might as well have not.

Eastern Whip-poor-will 

King Rail 

We whipped the van on outta the Keys and over to Fort My-ers, where we were invited to meet the king and queen of bird listing. They gave us a fantastic interview and got our ears tuned in to these elusive birds. For that, we are grateful.

White-crowned
Pigeon
Magnificent
Frigatebird
Mitred
Parakeet
f.
Eastern
Whip-poor-will
Clapper
Rail
King
Rail

Rollin' With Rolando

 A real Florida man contacted us and offered to take us out birdwatching. His name was Rolando. If it weren't for Rolando, we might've considered never setting foot in Florida again. These Midwestern boys just aren't built for it. I can't say enough good things about Rolando and his family—although his kid is a little menace. They were all extremely welcoming, cool, and knowledgeable as he*ck. We showed up one evening and they let us sleep inside on the couches and wash our dirty a*sses. They gave us beer, weed, and deer meat. The next day, Rolando took us down to Flamingo in the Everglades, where we launched his skiff into Florida Bay and headed to a place called Snake Bight. This is where we'd get redemption on flamingos. On the way there, we saw hundreds of wading birds—species we'd already seen, but now it felt like we were seeing them properly. We spotted a group of about 40 flamingos, and Rolando weaseled the skiff through a channel to get us a little closer. The tide wasn't in our favor, so we could only get within a couple hundred yards—just slightly closer than earlier in the year. But then suddenly, they all took flight and came directly our way. They flew right past the boat, giving us the look of a lifetime.

Cape May Warbler

More like the Cape Ga*y Warbler. Right, guys?

Grey Kingbird

More like the Ga*y Kingbird. Right?

Prairie Warbler

Hanging out in the mangroves, far, far away from any prairie.

Bananaquit

 To cap off a long day, Rolando drove us over an hour to a nature center in North Miami, where the rare vagrant had been seen every day for a week. We walked around and waited for it to show up. While doing so, we met a man who had flown in all the way from Tucson to see it. Just as we were about to banana-give-up, the little bird showed itself.

Cape May Warbler
f./im.
Grey Kingbird
Prairie Warbler
m.
flamingos
Bananaquit

Texas Again

Groove-billed Ani

In Biloxi, Mississippi, we found a single Ani hanging out next to some train tracks. A little later, I started to feel sick. We'd been driving across the coast for two days, and I thought some movement might help, so we drove to a local park to shoot hoops. Some local kids showed up and challenged us to a 2v2. They were probably only 12, but they were little menaces. They played aggressively and used bad words too often. After digging ourselves a 0–6 hole, we rebounded. I started finding net—I was having my flu game. We tied it up, but eventually the little fu*ckers won on a lucky shot. After that, we had to sleep in a Cracker Barrel parking lot. I was sweaty, fevery, and it was still 85 degrees. I ran a fan in the van so we could at least have moving air. I had the same fever dream all night long about an old woman pointing out a Turkey Vulture. In the morning, the van battery was dead, of course, and I was now very sick. This was a low point of the year.

Lesser Black-backed Gull

Back at Bolivar Flats on the way down to the RGV, we picked this bird out of a mixed flock of gulls and terns. We saw the same white SUV still parked in the spot it had been 10 months ago. This time, there was a person next to it. I could see some repetitive motion from afar—I thought maybe he was trying to fix the vehicle, so I took a quick look through the spotting scope. He wasn't fixing the vehicle, but he was fully naked and pleasuring himself. See: Iceland Gull.

Hooded Warbler

Hooded means uncircumcised as far as I know.

Ferruginous Pygmy Owl

 A couple local dudes—who were basically doppelgängers of the owl boys in Washington—offered to get us on this bird one evening. We met them in a grocery store parking lot, where I distracted the security guard so Owen could interview them. That guy took his job too seriously. The dudes were great birders, and relatively chill for being so into it. Respect.

Groove-billed
Ani
Lesser
Black-backed
Gull
Hooded
Warbler
Ferruginous
Pygmy Owl

Back in The RGV

Green Kingfisher

By far the hardest kingfisher for us to find. We'd tried several times in southeast Arizona and south Texas, but it eluded us each time. We must have been trying too hard, or the bird gods thought we just weren't ready yet. We finally found a pair at a wetland area in Edinburg, TX. They have huge bills compared to their small bodies.

Buff-bellied Hummingbird

Buff is another way to say brown. This was the last new term for brown we learned, and the last hummingbird we saw for the year. We went back to Bentsen-Rio Grande Valley State Park to see if anything had improved in the last 10 months. We still couldn't get a bike, it was still hot as di*ck, but we paid the $5 each and gave the showers another chance. More cockroaches than ever before, and the water was still *buff*. The only cool part was when the guy with face tattoos picked us up in one of those limousine golf carts and drove us around the park. That guy rules.

Clay-colored Thrush

Clay comes in many different colors, so yeah, of course it is.

Fulvous Whistling Duck

Closest thing we saw to a Blue-footed Booby all year—and I was kinda disappointed about that.

Morelet's Seedeater

 More or less a seed eater. Small bird—quite small. Short, stubby little bill. They're really only seen in the grasses along the Rio Grande in South Texas. They're considered rare in the United States—a code of three or higher. This means that if people are subscribed to rare bird alerts, they'll get an email about it. Two idiots find a little brown bird, and now they're in your inbox. Isn't that something.

Green
Kingfisher
m.
Buff-bellied
Hummingbird
Clay-colored
Thrush
Fulvous
Whistling
Duck
Morelet's
Seedeater
f.
seed

One Last Dance

Late December

Duration: 6 days
Distance: 1,992mi
New Birds: 5
Total Birds: 579
Cracker Barrel Stays: 1

General Route: North to Madison and Duluth and the Sax-Zim bog, then over to Sturgeon Bay, then back south through Chicago, returning to Southern Illinois.

Significant Places: Sax-Zim Bog, Hibbing, Duluth, Sturgeon Bay.

Weather: Cold, but not cold enough.

Overview

It had been well over a month since we got back from our last trip. We'd debated going to the East Coast for a while. We'd done the math, and if we saw every possible bird up there, we could likely make it to 600 species on the year, which would've been a huge accomplishment for us. We thought about navigating the big conglomerate of cities, as well as the poor sleep we'd likely get. That was enough to abandon the idea.

There were, however, a few birds left on the table around Minnesota. We'd had such a good time there earlier in the year, we figured we would just head back up there, play some pond hockey, and add a couple more birds to the list to finish 'er out.

It was forecasted to be an *irruption* year for Boreal Owls, but it turned out that we were still a bit early for that. They make their way south to the United States a little later in the winter, when it gets too cold farther north. It was too early for them, and slightly too warm for pond hockey. The McDavitt Park rink was slushy, and only portions were skatable. It still proved to be an enjoyable outing, and this time we found a Great Grey Owl on our own, without secretly following a birding guide van.

On the 30th, we saw a rare bird had been reported a few hundred miles away, but within a day's drive. We thought it would only be right to end it on that. We drove the rest of the day, from the bog to Sturgeon Bay. The next morning, on the last day of the year, we capped it all off by standing with a crowd of weirdos and watching a lost bird from a different continent.

The Final Five

Long-eared Owl

 Someone has to let you in on the secret of where they might be hiding. Their locations aren't visible on the bird software because they're considered a sensitive species. In winter, they roost in stands of trees surrounded by large open areas for hunting. Some nice people had whispered in our ear about several different potential locations throughout the year, but each time we were turned away. At one spot, we were too late. At another, the vegetation was too thick. At yet another, there was an active grizzly bear den—and that's just not worth it. We did finally find one in Minnesota, thanks to Sparky.

White-winged Crossbill

When compared to the Red Crossbill, you'll notice this one has two white wing bars on each wing. See: Red Crossbill.

Lapland Longspur

 We looked for these fancy sparrows many times throughout the year. The name sounds British, so we assumed they were redcoats. We eventually found an army of about 70 in a farm field.

American Black Duck

A dark chocolate duck. This duck is common, but it just eluded us for the whole year—or at least we thought it had. I looked back at my images from early January and found that I'd actually photographed one on the first day without even noticing. We could've gone back and counted it, but being the men of integrity that we are, we decided we needed to find one for real.

White Wagtail

 Mostly whitish, ground-dwelling bird. Constantly wags its tail. On the final day of the year, we found ourselves at one last rare bird stakeout in Sturgeon Bay, Wisconsin. We'd driven most of the day before for the chance at one more bird—and one more opportunity to see the weirdos that chase them. Of course, over the year, we'd become some of those weirdos—but only sort of.

Long-eared Owl
White-winged Crossbill
m.
Lapland Longspur
nb.
American Black Duck
m.
White Wagtail
in flight

These Data Suggest

579 species
It's a lot of birds no matter how you draw it up.

38,757mi
Roughly 16% of the way to the Moon.

42 Cracker Barrels
The one on Bass Pro Drive in Harlingen, Texas, takes the cake—hosting us for a total of 10 nights throughout the year.

~400 cans of Tuna
Why are my arms numb?

~$16,000 USD
A wise man once told us that when you do a big year, you need to think about your cost per bird—or *CPB*. By living in a minivan, we'd kept our CPB pretty low (~$27 USD). But we came to learn that cost is not always monetary. There were many times where we just didn't have the mustard. Times where we didn't feel like being in a busy city, or times where we didn't feel like picking through a thousand seagulls to see if there was one that was slightly different. We did what was worth it to us.

Notable Misses
As novices, we missed a lot of common birds, and you unfortunately won't find them in this book. Here are a few notable ones:

Black-billed Cuckoo	Canada Warbler
Swallow-tailed Kite	Connecticut Warbler
Philadelphia Vireo	Kirtland's Warbler
Henslow's Sparrow	Black Scoter
Greater Pewee	Wilson's Plover
Rosy Finches	Gunnison Sage Grouse
Prairie Chickens	Dusky Grouse
Snow Bunting	Sooty Grouse
Spotted Owl	Spruce Grouse
Boreal Owl	LeConte's Thrasher
Boreal Chickadee	Bendire's Thrasher
Mangrove Cuckoo	Antillean Nighthawk
Northern Gannet	

What Was All That About?

We will never do a big year again, but I'm glad we did. Neither of us are competitive birdwatchers. It doesn't resonate with me, and it doesn't tickle Owen's fancy, but it was good to participate. I think bird listing can be a great outlet for some folks—there are far worse hobbies.

For us, as the year went on, we were increasingly just in it for the good times. We spent a lot of time birdwatching, but an equal or greater amount of time fu*cking off. As I look back, I realize we were really just looking for a good reason to go on a road trip. Having a quest is always good, and this bird shi*t is undeniably hilarious. I'm now convinced that there is no better way to see this country than to go searching for birds. I'm also convinced that this is the greatest country on Earth.

Owen and I are birdwatchers now, it's as simple as that. It's an incurable disease. It all happened so fast, and it could happen to you too if you're not careful. We don't make a list of every bird we encounter, or even seek out specific birds, but we pay attention to them everywhere we go. Mentally noting what we're hearing and seeing—something neither of us did before. If we learned anything, it's that when you pay attention to birds, you pay attention to a lot of other stuff as well.

Supplementary Material

 - Movie

 - Instagram

 - ???

Index

****

References

Cornell Lab of Ornithology (online)
eBird
Merlin
All About Birds

Golden Field Guide (Blue)
A Guide to Field Identification Birds of North America

Big Orange National Audubon Society Bird Book
Birds of North America